AAT

DEVOLVED ASSESSMENT
KIT

Intermediate Unit 21

Using Information Technology

In this August 2000 edition

- Activities designed to teach you the skills required to complete **Devolved Assessment** tasks

- Four **Practice Devolved Assessments** to help you get up to speed

- Three **Trial Run Devolved Assessments**

- The **AAT's Sample Simulation** for this Unit

- **Data files on CD-ROM** (with solutions) for the more complex Activities and Assessments, and for the AAT's Sample Simulation

FOR 2000 AND 2001 DEVOLVED ASSESSMENTS

BPP Publishing
August 2000

First edition 1998
Third edition August 2000

ISBN 0 7517 6240 7 (previous edition 0 7517 6173 7)

British Library Cataloguing-in-Publication Data
A catalogue record for this book
is available from the British Library

Published by

BPP Publishing Limited
Aldine House, Aldine Place
London W12 8AW

www.bpp.com

Printed in Great Britain by Ashford Colour Print

We are grateful to the Lead Body for Accounting for permission to reproduce extracts from the Standards of Competence for Accounting.

Contents

BPP
PUBLISHING

HOW TO USE THIS DEVOLVED ASSESSMENT KIT

Aims of this Devolved Assessment Kit

> To provide the knowledge and practice to help you succeed in the devolved assessment for Intermediate Unit 21 *Using Information Technology*.

To pass the devolved assessment you need a thorough understanding in all areas covered by the standards of competence.

> To tie in with the other components of the BPP Effective Study Package to ensure you have the best possible chance of success.

Interactive Text
This covers all you need to know for devolved assessment for Unit 21 *Using Information Technology*. Icons clearly mark key areas of the text. Numerous activities throughout the text help you practise what you have just learnt.

Devolved Assessment Kit
When you have understood and practised the material in the Interactive Text, you will have the knowledge and experience to tackle this Devolved Assessment Kit for Unit 21 *Using Information Technology*. This aims to get you through the devolved assessment, whether in the form of a simulation or workplace assessment. It contains the AAT's sample simulation for Unit 21 plus other simulations.

RECOMMENDED APPROACH TO THIS DEVOLVED ASSESSMENT KIT

- To achieve competence in all units you need to be able to do **everything** specified by the standards. Study the Interactive Text very carefully and do not skip any of it.

- Learning is an **active** process. Do **all** the activities as you work through the Interactive Text so you can be sure you really understand what you have read.

- After you have covered the material in the Interactive Text, work through this **Devolved Assessment Kit**.

- Try the **Practice Activities** first. These are short activities, linked into each part of the Interactive Text, to reinforce your learning and consolidate the practice that you have had doing the activities in the Interactive Text.

- Then attempt the Practice Devolved Assessment. They are designed to test your competence in certain key areas of the Standards of Competence, but are not as comprehensive as the ones set by the AAT. They are a 'warm-up' exercise, to develop your studies towards the level of full Devolved Assessment.

- Next do the **Trial Run Devolved assessments**. These cover all the performance criteria of the elements indicated.

- Finally try the AAT's **Sample Simulation,** which gives you the clearest idea of what a full assessment will be like.

Remember this is a **practical** course.

- Try to relate the material to your experience in the workplace or any other work experience you may have had.

- Try to make as many links as you can to your study of the other Units at Intermediate level.

HOW TO USE THE BPP UNIT 21 CD-ROM

The CD-ROM that is shrink-wrapped with new copies of this book contains **data** that you will need to complete some of the longer or more complex tasks in this book. Spreadsheet data is provided in **Microsoft Excel** format, database data is in **Microsoft Access** format.

To make use of this data **you need:**

- **A CD-ROM drive**

- **Microsoft Windows 95/98/2000 or Windows NT**

- **Microsoft Excel 97 or above – to use the 30 spreadsheet files**

- **Microsoft Access 97 or above – to use the 2 database files**

Installation

The data on the CD-ROM needs to be installed on your computer's hard drive. Follow the instructions below.

Either...
From the taskbar click on **Start** and select **Run.** In the pop-up box type **D:\BPPU21** and click **OK. (This assumes your CD-ROM drive is drive D, if your CD-ROM drive has been assigned a different letter use that.)** Then click on **OK** in the pop-up box.

Or...
View the CD-ROM in Windows Explorer and **double-click** on the **BppU21.exe** file. Then click on **OK** in the pop-up box.

If you see the following message the files are being **extracted to C:\BPPU21** and **you do not need to do anything**.

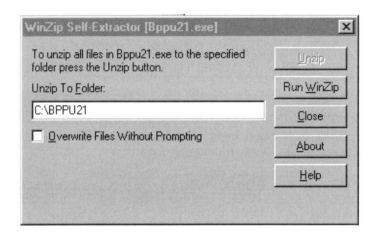

File already exists

If you see a message like the one below, the data has **already been installed** on your computer.

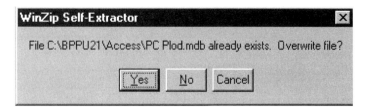

Click **Yes** to overwrite the file specified with a new version. Click **No** if you want to keep your current version of the file (for instance if you have made changes to it but saved it under its original name). New files that you have created with different names will not be affected.

What next?

If you have followed the instructions above the data has been copied into a directory on your hard drive called **C:\BPPU21**. (You may need to press the **F5** key to refresh your screen before you can see this directory in Windows Explorer.)

If you look at this directory using Windows Explorer you will find that it has two subdirectories.

(a)   One contains 30 spreadsheet files in **Microsoft Excel** format.
(b)   The other contains 2 database files in **Microsoft Access** format.

Opening and saving the files

If you make any changes to the files provided by BPP you should **save** your modified file with a **new name**. That way you keep both a clean copy of the original and your own modified file.

If you accidentally modify a BPP file and then want a fresh copy of the original you can get one by **reinstalling** the data from the CD-ROM.

Passwords

Some of the files contain **solutions** to some of the exercises and assessments in this book. These files are **password protected**, to encourage you to have a reasonable attempt at the tasks you are expected to do rather than copying our answer.

The passwords to open the files containing solutions will be found **within the written solutions** to the relevant tasks in this book, on the assumption that if you are looking at the solution you have already attempted the task.

Security

You should keep the CD-ROM that accompanies the BPP AAT Unit 21 Devolved Assessment Kit safely. If you need a replacement you will have to convince our sales staff that you purchased a new copy of the book!

UNIT 21 STANDARDS OF COMPETENCE

Unit 21: Using Information Technology

What is the unit about?

This unit is about using information technology as an essential tool when undertaking accounting activities. It involves being able to obtain any required information from the Management Information System (MIS) and being able to produce spreadsheets for the analysis and presentation of numerical information. The candidate has responsibility for observing the Data Protection Act, obtaining information from the MIS and correctly manipulating it in spreadsheets. Their responsibility extends to obtaining authorisation for its use, keeping confidential information secure and evaluating its appropriateness. The candidate will also be required to evaluate the quality of the MIS whilst using it and make appropriate recommendations for its improvement.

Elements contained within this unit are:

Element: 21.1   Obtain information from a computerised Management Information System

Element: 21.2   Produce spreadsheets for the analysis of numerical information

Element: 21.3   Contribute to the quality of the Management Information System

Knowledge and understanding

General information technology

- Purpose and application of MIS (Elements 21.1 & 21.3)

- Relationship between MIS and other IT applications (Elements 21.1, 21.2 & 21.3)

- Range of MIS used in organisations (Element 21.1 & 21.3)

- A range of spreadsheet products (Element 21.2)

- Interfaces with other software packages: databases, word processors (Element 21.2)

- Purpose and application of spreadsheets (Element 21.2)

The organisation

- Types of information contained within the MIS (Elements 21.1, 21.2 & 21.3)

- Location of information sources (Elements 21.1, 21.2 & 21.3)

- Ways of organising, interpreting and presenting information (Elements 21.1 & 21.3)

- Relevant security and legal regulations, including the Data Protection Act, and their purpose (Elements 21.1, 21.2 & 21.3)

- Organisations' computer software, systems and networking (Elements 21.1 & 21.3)

- Cost benefit analysis techniques (Element 21.3)

Element 21.1: Obtain information from a computerised Management Information System

Performance criteria

1   The required information is correctly located within the MIS structure

2   Advice is sought where there are difficulties in obtaining the required information

3   Additional authorisation is obtained for sensitive or confidential information in accordance with the organisation's security regulations

4   Information is checked for its accuracy and completeness

5   Information is stored in a format which helps others to access it and use it

6   Confidential information is kept secure and not disclosed to unauthorised people

Range statement

1   Information locations: database; unique reference codes

2   Information: obtained for own work and area of responsibility; obtained on request from others

3   Difficulties: costs incurred; time taken

Evidence requirements

• Competence must be demonstrated consistently, over an appropriate timescale with evidence of performance being provided from obtaining information from an organisation's MIS or part of an organisation's MIS

Sources of evidence (these are examples of sources of evidence, but candidates and assessors may be able to identify other, appropriate sources)

Observed performance, eg

-   Obtaining information from an MIS

-   Seeking advice

-   Explore more cost effective methods of obtaining data

-   Evaluating information

-   Presenting information

Work produced by candidate, eg

-   Advice that has been given

-   Notification of methods not being cost effective

-   Authorisation for information

-   Print-outs obtained from the MIS

Authenticated testimonies from relevant witnesses

Personal accounts of competence, eg

-   Report of performance

Other sources of evidence to prove competence or knowledge and understanding where it is not apparent from performance, eg

-   Reports and working papers

-   Performance in simulation

-   Responses to questions

Element 21.2: Produce spreadsheets for the analysis of numerical information

Performance criteria

1   The spreadsheet is titled in a way which clearly defines its use and purpose

2   The arrangement of the spreadsheet is consistent with organisational conventions

3   All rates and other numeric inputs and assumptions are stated to the correct number of decimal places

4   Calculated values are checked for correctness when changes are made to the inputs

5   The spreadsheet is used to carry out data modifications and for entry of related formulas

6   Each cell is formatted clearly and accurately

7   A method is selected to eliminate rounding errors which is suitable for the purpose of the spreadsheet

8   Confidential information is kept secure and not disclosed to unauthorised people

Range statement

1   Spreadsheets produced by: modification; creation

2   Spreadsheets: which require possible rounding errors; which have conditions in some formulae; which are used to produce graphs

3   Spreadsheet produced: for own work and area of responsibility; on request from others

4   Information: numeric; alphabetic

Evidence requirements

•   Competence must be demonstrated consistently, with evidence of performance being provided from the production of the full range of spreadsheets in one organisational MIS or part of an organisation's MIS

Sources of evidence (these are examples of sources of evidence, but candidates and assessors may be able to identify other, appropriate sources)

    Observed performance, eg

-   Inputting data on a spreadsheet
-   Checking calculated values
-   Modifying data
-   Entering related formulas
-   Eliminating rounding errors

    Work produced by candidate, eg

-   Formatted spreadsheets

    Authenticated testimonies from relevant witnesses

    Personal accounts of competence, eg

-   Report of performance

    Other sources of evidence to prove competence or knowledge and understanding where it is not apparent from performance, eg

-   Performance in simulation
-   Performance in independent assessment
-   Responses to verbal questioning

Element 21.3: Contribute to the quality of the Management Information System

Performance criteria

1   Potential improvements to the MIS are identified and considered for their impact on the quality of the system and any interrelated systems

2   Suggestions for changes are supported by a clear rationale as to how they could improve the quality of the system

3   The reliability of assumptions and judgements made is assessed and clearly stated

4   The benefits and costs of all changes are described accurately

5   Suggestions are presented clearly and in a way which helps people to understand and act on them

Range statement

1   MIS: computerised system

Evidence requirements

•   Competence must be demonstrated consistently over an appropriate timescale, with evidence of performance being provided from involvement with an organisation's MIS or part of an organisation's MIS

Sources of evidence (these are examples of sources of evidence, but candidates and assessors may be able to identify other, appropriate sources)

Observed performance, eg

-   Evaluating an MIS

-   Calculating benefits and costs

-   Presenting suggestions

Work produced by candidate, eg

-   Report of suggestions

-   Rationale for suggestions

-   Descriptions of costs and benefits

-   Correspondence relating to the MIS

-   Minutes from meetings

-   Suggestions made

Authenticated testimonies from relevant witnesses

Personal accounts of competence, eg

-   Report of performance

Other sources of evidence to prove competence or knowledge and understanding where it is not apparent from performance, eg

-   Performance in simulation

-   Responses to verbal questioning

ASSESSMENT STRATEGY

This Unit is assessed entirely by means of **Devolved Assessment**.

Devolved Assessment

Devolved Assessment is a means of collecting evidence of your ability to carry out practical activities and to operate effectively in the conditions of the workplace to the standards required. Evidence may be collected at your place of work, or at an Approved Assessment Centre by means of simulations of workplace activity, or by a combination of these methods.

If the Approved Assessment Centre is a workplace, you may be observed carrying out accounting activities as part of your normal work routine. You should collect documentary evidence of the work you have done, or contributed to, in an **accounting portfolio**. Evidence collected in a portfolio can be assessed in addition to observed performance or where it is not possible to assess by observation.

Where the Approved Assessment Centre is a **college or training organisation**, devolved assessment will be by means of a combination of the following.

- Documentary evidence of activities carried out at the workplace, collected by you in an **accounting portfolio**.

- Realistic **simulations** of workplace activities. These simulations may take the form of case studies and in-tray exercises and involve the use of primary documents and reference sources.

- **Projects and assignments** designed to assess the Standards of Competence.

If you are unable to provide workplace evidence you will be able to complete the assessment requirements by the alternative methods listed above.

Possible assessment methods

Where possible, evidence should be collected in the workplace, but this may not be a practical prospect for you. Equally, where workplace evidence can be gathered it may not cover all elements. The AAT regards performance evidence from simulations, case studies, projects and assignments as an acceptable substitute for performance at work, provided that they are based on the Standards and, as far as possible, on workplace practice.

There are a number of methods of assessing competence. The list on the following two pages is not exhaustive, nor is it prescriptive. Some methods have limited applicability, but others are capable of being expanded to provide challenging tests of competence.

Assessment method	Suitable for assessing
Performance of an accounting task either in the workplace or by simulation: eg preparing and processing documents, posting entries, making adjustments, balancing, calculating, analysing information etc by manual or computerised processes	**Basic task competence.** Adding supplementary oral questioning may help to draw out underpinning knowledge and understanding and highlight your ability to deal with contingencies and unexpected occurrences
General case studies. These are broader than simulations. They include more background information about the system and business environment	Ability to **analyse a system** and suggest ways of modifying it. It could take the form of a written report, with or without the addition of oral or written questions
Accounting problems/cases: eg a list of balances that require adjustments and the preparation of final accounts	Understanding of the **general principles of accounting** as applied to a particular case or topic
Preparation of flowcharts/diagrams. To illustrate an actual (or simulated) accounting procedure	**Understanding of the logic** behind a procedure, of controls, and of relationships between departments and procedures. Questions on the flow chart or diagram can provide evidence of underpinning knowledge and understanding
Interpretation of accounting information from an actual or simulated situation. The assessment could include non-financial information and written or oral questioning	**Interpretative competence**
Preparation of written reports on an actual or simulated situation	**Written communication skills**
Analysis of critical incidents, problems encountered, achievements	Your ability to handle **contingencies**
Listing of likely errors eg preparing a list of the main types of errors likely to occur in an actual or simulated procedure	Appreciation of the range of **contingencies** likely to be encountered. Oral or written questioning would be a useful supplement to the list
Outlining the organisation's policies, guidelines and regulations	Performance criteria relating to these aspects of competence. It also provides evidence of competence in **researching information**
Objective tests and short-answer questions	**Specific knowledge**
In-tray exercises	Your **task-management ability** as well as technical competence
Supervisors' reports	**General job competence,** personal effectiveness, reliability, accuracy, and time management. Reports need to be related specifically to the Standards of Competence
Analysis of work logbooks/diaries	**Personal effectiveness,** time management etc. It may usefully be supplemented with oral questioning

Assessment method	Suitable for assessing
Formal written answers to questions	Knowledge and understanding of the **general accounting environment** and its impact on particular units of competence
Oral questioning	**Knowledge and understanding** across the range of competence including organisational procedures, methods of dealing with unusual cases, contingencies and so on. It is often used in conjunction with other methods

Practice Activities

Activity 1   Level: MODERATE

Open the spreadsheet **Ac_01_Q** which was provided on the CD-ROM that came with this book. (If you have not installed these files yet, do so now. See pages (vi) and (vii).)

You will find the file in the directory **C:\BPPU21\EXCEL** on your hard drive.

You will see a spreadsheet like the following.

	A	B	C	D	E	F
1						
2						
3			**Name**	Paula		
4			**Age**	24		
5						
6						
7						
8						
9						
10			**Name**	**Age**		
11			Annette	38		
12			Josephine	43		
13			Mike	32		
14			Paula	24		
15						

Type one of the names in cells C11 to C14 in the name box (cell D3) and press Enter. What happens, and why?

Activity 2   Level: MODERATE

Open the spreadsheet **Ac_02_Q** from the Excel sub-directory of your BPPU21 directory. The sheet will look like illustration below.

It shows how much accountants of different grades are paid in an audit firm and the hours over a two week period they spent working on the audit of a particular client. Accountants are identified by a four character personnel number such as Q001.

Practice activities

	A	B	C	D	E	F	G	H
1	Grade	Chargeout Rate (£/hour)			Employee	Grade	Hours	
2	1	20.00			Q021	3	7	
3	2	17.50			P004	1	20	
4	3	16.00			P004	1	5	
5	4	14.25			P004	1	29	
6	5	12.50			P007	3	9	
7					U003	4	7	
8					D022	3	30	
9					D022	3	15	
10					P007	3	15	
11					P012	2	19	
12					Q001	5	19	
13					F001	5	3	
14					C015	4	14	
15					C015	4	28	
16					Q005	3	17	
17					F001	5	2	
18					Q001	5	16	
19					U011	2	30	
20					A047	3	1	
21					A047	3	34	
22					Q021	3	7	
23					U002	2	20	
24					U011	2	15	
25					Q021	3	13	
26					P004	1	8	
27					Q021	3	19	
28					P012	2	9	
29					U003	4	17	
30					Q005	3	29	
31					U002	2	26	
32								

Using the skill you learned in Activity 1, calculate the total to bill this client for the audit work done.

Activity 3

Level: MODERATE

You work for a business called Dunraven. You are faced with the task of producing the trial balance at the end of the year to 30 June 20X6. You decide to use a spreadsheet, building it up from scratch this year, in order to save time in future years. The following balances have been extracted from the ledgers.

	£
Sales	336,247
Purchases	224,362
Carriage	6,184
Drawings	14,686
Rent and rates	14,621
Postage and stationery	5,789
Advertising	2,941
Salaries and wages	56,934
Bad debt expense	1,614
Provision for bad debts	365
Debtors	31,050
Creditors	9,456
Cash in hand	422
Cash at bank	2,136
Stock as at 1 July 20X5	15,605
Equipment: at cost	116,000
accumulated depreciation	55,400
Capital	90,876

The following additional information comes to light.

(a) Of the carriage costs, £1,624 represents carriage inwards on purchases.

(b) Rates are payable 6 months in advance. A payment of £2,120 made on 30 June 20X6 represents rates for July to December 20X7.

(c) A rent demand for £510 for the three months ended 30 June 20X6 was not received until 1 July 20X6.

(d) Equipment is to be depreciated at 15% per annum using the straight line method.

(e) The provision for bad debts is to be increased to 2% of debtors.

(f) Closing stock was £31,529.

Task

Prepare an extended trial balance using a spreadsheet package.

Activity 4   Level: EASY

At the last minute you decide to change the depreciation rate for equipment to 20% per annum straight line method.

Task

Update your spreadsheet in Activity 3 to reflect this change of policy, which will not affect prior years.

Activity 5   Level: MODERATE

The following balances were extracted from the ledger accounts of Oaklands, a trader, at 31 December 20X4. These figures are available already entered for you in the file **Ac_05_Q** in your BPP data.

	£
Freehold land and buildings	25,000
Furniture & fittings: cost	3,360
accumulated depreciation	2,016
Motor car: cost	1,900
accumulated depreciation	980
Trade debtors	16,121
Trade creditors	9,125
Bank	4,873
Provision for doubtful debts at 1.1.20X4	792
Stock at 1.1.20X4	10,858
Sales	142,125
Purchases	101,286
Rent received	810
Car expenses	841
Bad debt expense	943
General expenses	1,842
Rent and rates	2,414
Wages and salaries	18,103
Discounts allowed	3,125
Capital	44,550
Drawings	9,732

BPP
PUBLISHING

Practice activities

You ascertain the following.

  (a) Stock at 31 December 20X4 was £12,654.

  (b) Rates paid in advance at 31 December 20X4 were £106.

  (c) It has been decided to reduce the provision for doubtful debts to 4% of debtors as at 31 December 20X4.

  (d) The tenant owes £268 in rent at 31 December 20X4.

  (e) Wages and salaries accrued at 31 December 20X4 were £421.

  (f) Depreciation is to be provided as for 20X3.

  (g) Unused stamps in the franking machine as at 31 December 20X4 amounted to £86.

Task

Using the file **Ac_05_Q**, or a copy of its data, prepare an extended trial balance as at 31 December 20X4.

Activity 6   Level: EASY

When you have completed the spreadsheet in Activity 5, there is a change of depreciation policy for the motor car. It is now proposed to provide depreciation at 25% on the reducing balance.

Task

Amend your spreadsheet accordingly.

Activity 7   Level: ADVANCED

In the spreadsheet below, only the cells A1 and A2 contain data. Cells B1:D2 contain formulae.

	A	B	C	D
1	23/02/2001	23	2	2001
2	31/12/2001	31	12	2001
3	311			

Task

What do you think the formulae are? (Use Excel's Help facility if necessary.) What is the result of subtracting cell A1 from cell A2?

Activity 8   Level: ADVANCED

Goodwood, a furniture-making business manufactures quality furniture to customers' orders. It has three production departments and two service departments. Budgeted overhead costs for the coming year, 20X6, are as follows.

	Total £
Rent and rates	12,800
Machine insurance	6,000
Telephone charges	3,200
Depreciation	18,000
Production supervisor	24,000
Heat and light	6,400
	70,400

The three production departments - A, B and C and the two service departments X and Y are housed in the new premises, the details of which, together with other statistics and information are given below.

	Departments				
	A	B	C	X	Y
Floor area occupied (sq metres)	3,000	1,800	600	600	400
Machine value (£'000s)	24	10	8	4	2
Direct labour hrs budgeted	3,200	1,800	1,000		
Labour rates per hour	£3.80	£3.50	£3.40	£3.00	£3.00
Allocated overheads					
Specific to each department (£'000s)	2.8	1.7	1.2	0.8	0.6
Service department X's costs apportioned	50%	25%	25%		
Service department Y's costs apportioned	20%	30%	50%		

Tasks

(a) Prepare a spreadsheet showing the overhead cost budgeted for each department. Use the following bases of apportionment.

Overhead item	*Basis of apportionment*
Allocated costs	Specific to dept
Rent and rates	Floor area
Machine insurance	Machine value
Telephone charges	Floor area
Depreciation	Machine value
Production supervisor	Direct labour hours
Heat and light	Floor area

(b) Calculate overhead absorption rates for each department based on direct labour hours.

Activity 9   Level: ADVANCED

The budgeted overheads in Activity 8 have been revised as follows.

Rent and rates	Up by 5%
Machine insurance	Up by 10%
Telephone charges	Up by 25%
Depreciation	Unchanged
Production supervision	Up by 2.8%
Heat and light	Down by 8%

Task

Amend your spreadsheet accordingly.

Activity 10   Level: EASY

(a) What is the best way to ensure that the formulae contained in a spreadsheet are accurate?

(b) Name two important facilities available in spreadsheets that can be used as controls.

(c) List three ways of ensuring that unauthorised persons do not gain access to confidential material in spreadsheets.

Activity 11   Level: EASY

(a) List six qualities of useful information.

(b) What factors need to be considered when deciding whether or not it is worth collecting information?

(c) What practical matters need to be taken into account when collecting information?

(d) What are the four main sources of information for use in spreadsheets?

Activity 12   Level: ADVANCED

Open the file **Ac_12_Q** in your BPP data. You will see a spreadsheet that looks like this (except that there are 100 rows of data).

	A	B	C	D
1	Issue No	Quantity	Colour	Shape
2	1473	159	Blue	Square
3	1474	84	Yellow	Square
4	1475	120	Green	Triangular
5	1476	125	Blue	Round
6	1477	153	Yellow	Triangular
7	1478	99	Blue	Round
8	1479	137	Blue	Triangular
9	1480	199	Red	Square
10	1481	16	Red	Round
11	1482	158	Green	Square
12	1483	29	Red	Triangular
13	1484	118	Yellow	Square
14	1485	167	Blue	Round
15	1486	177	Red	Triangular
16	1487	168	Green	Square
17	1488	110	Red	Round
18	1489	181	Red	Square
19	1490	168	Blue	Square
20	1491	31	Red	Square
21	1492	86	Green	Triangular
22	1493	160	Green	Triangular
23	1494	120	Red	Square
24	1495	101	Blue	Triangular
25	1496	141	Red	Triangular
26	1497	187	Blue	Triangular
27	1498	62	Green	Square
28	1499	177	Blue	Triangular
29	1500	148	Green	Square
30	1501	175	Red	Triangular
31	1502	131	Red	Square
32	1503	67	Blue	Square
33	1504	18	Blue	Round

The spreadsheet shows the quantity of components of various types that were issued from stores to production during a period. Components come in four colours (Blue, Red, Green and Yellow) and three shapes (Square, Round and Triangular).

You have decided to learn how to use Microsoft Excel's Pivot Table feature to analyse and summarise this data. You are given step by step instructions below.

Tasks

(a) Position the cursor anywhere in columns A to D and rows 1 to 100, for instance in cell A1 or cell C24.

(b) Click on **Data** in the menu bar at the top of the screen. Select the **Pivot Table Report** option.

(c) The following screen will appear. Make sure that the option Microsoft Excel or data base is selected and the click on **Next>**.

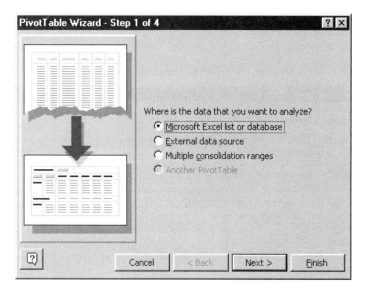

(d) The following Window will appear. The Range you want to base your Pivot Table on is already filled in for you because you positioned your cursor within it at step (a), so you can just click on **Next>**.

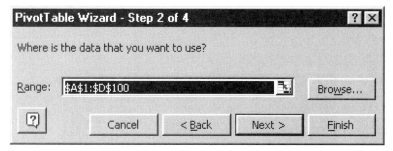

(e) The following screen will appear. This is the point at which people usually give up with Pivot Tables because they don't understand what to do next. You are not going to give up.

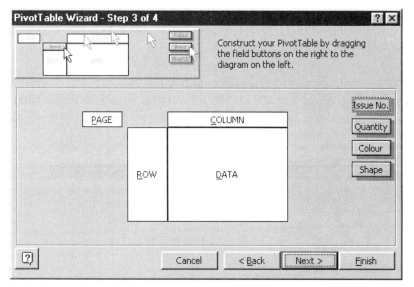

Left-click on the button labelled **Shape,** and keeping your left mouse button held down drag the button into the white space labelled ROW. A copy of the Shape button will be created there.

Do like wise with the button labelled **Colour** except drag it to the white space labelled COLUMN.

Do likewise with the button labelled **Quantity** but drag it into the white space labelled DATA.

Your screen will now look something like this.

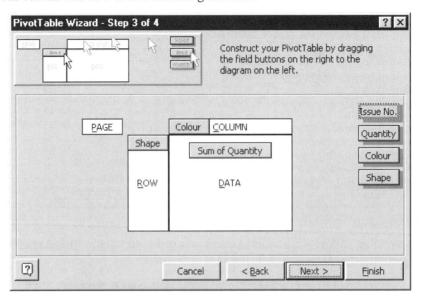

(f)   Click on the button labelled **Sum of Quantity.** A pop-up Window will appear as follows.

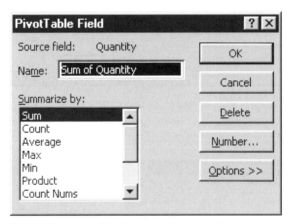

Select the word **Product** in the Summarize by: list box and watch the entry in the Name box change. In fact the option we want on this occasion is **Sum,** so select **Sum** again in the list box to make the screen look exactly like it does above. Click on **OK.**

(g)   In the main screen click on **Next>.** The following screen will appear.

Choose the option to put the Pivot Table in a **New worksheet** and click on Finish.

The result will be as follows.

	A	B	C	D	E	F
1	Sum of Quantity	Colour				
2	Shape	Blue	Green	Red	Yellow	Grand Total
3	Round	482	584	297	824	2187
4	Square	628	1440	1240	1153	4461
5	Triangular	1195	1139	1114	782	4230
6	Grand Total	2305	3163	2651	2759	10878
7						
8						
9						

This summarises quantities of components used by shape and colour: exactly what you wanted to do, with the click of a few buttons!

(h) Select the cell C4 (the total of square green components issued) and double click on it. The following will appear in a new sheet.

	A	B	C	D
1	Issue No.	Quantity	Colour	Shape
2	1559	68	Green	Square
3	1553	200	Green	Square
4	1550	138	Green	Square
5	1548	68	Green	Square
6	1533	63	Green	Square
7	1524	115	Green	Square
8	1519	108	Green	Square
9	1516	144	Green	Square
10	1500	148	Green	Square
11	1482	158	Green	Square
12	1498	62	Green	Square
13	1487	168	Green	Square
14				

Here you have **drilled down** to find the issue note information underlying the total of 1,440 issues of square green components.

(i) Return to the Pivot table sheet and drag the button labelled **Colour** (in cell B1) into cell A3. The data will instantly be rearranged as follows.

	A	B	C	D
1	Sum of Quantity			
2	Colour	Shape	Total	
3	Blue	Round	482	
4		Square	628	
5		Triangular	1195	
6	Blue Total		2305	
7	Green	Round	584	
8		Square	1440	
9		Triangular	1139	
10	Green Total		3163	
11	Red	Round	297	
12		Square	1240	
13		Triangular	1114	
14	Red Total		2651	
15	Yellow	Round	824	
16		Square	1153	
17		Triangular	782	
18	Yellow Total		2759	
19	Grand Total		10878	
20				

11

(j) Play with the Pivot table some more before you close it. For instance try right clicking within it and experimenting with some of the other options. (For instance the Wizard option lets you go back to the **Step 3 of 4** where you choose your layout. What is the effect of other choices of buttons and other layouts? Can you just have a button in the DATA area without specifying Row or Column? As another experiment, find out what happens to your Pivot Table if you alter the figures in the original data).

(k) Create a copy of the original data in a fresh sheet and see if you can construct a Pivot Table on your own without looking at these instructions.

Activity 13   Level: ADVANCED

The accountant at Rolling Projections Ltd is preparing the cash flow forecast for the coming year. She has projected what she thinks the opening balance sheet (at 01 July 20X5) will be and wishes to prepare a 12 month (monthly) forecast.

The following information is relevant.

(a) PROJECTED OPENING BALANCE SHEET

	£'000	£'000
Land and buildings	220	
Plant and machinery	110	
Motor vehicles	65	
		395
Stock	40	
Trade debtors	60	
Cash in hand	5	
	105	
Overdraft	65	
Trade creditors	35	
	100	
Net current assets		5
Long term creditors		120
Net assets		280
Share capital		100
Reserves		180
		280

(b) BUDGETED PROFIT AND LOSS ACCOUNT
    FOR THE YEAR ENDING 30 JUNE 20X6

	£'000
Sales	390
Cost of sales	165
Rent and rates	60
Depreciation	30
Marketing	35
Administrative expenses	75
Selling expenses	45
Loss before interest	20

(c) One sixth of the year's sales occur in each of the months of July and August. The rest are evenly spread over the remaining months of the year. Debtor balances are usually collected as follows.

10% in the month of sale
60% in the month following sale
30% in the second month after sale

The accountant expects to be able to collect 90% of opening debtor balances in July and will write off the rest.

(d) Trade creditors are paid 20% in the month of purchase and 80% in the following month. Because she ran a large batch of cheques just before year end, the accountant does not expect to have to settle opening trade creditors until August.

The accountant is budgeting for no overall change in stock levels. Purchases are spread evenly over the year.

(e) Rates, which total £20,000, are paid in April, and rent (the balance on the rent and rates account) is paid in equal amounts on the Quarter Days.

(f) The marketing budget is set at £1,000 per month excluding November. The balance will be spent on a major burst campaign in November.

(g) Administrative expenses are spread evenly over the year.

(h) Selling expenses are paid in the month of sale and are incurred in the same proportion as that in which sales are earned.

(i) Interest of 2% per month is paid on any overdraft balance at the end of the month and added to the account balance. (Hint: use an IF function.)

(j) Cash in hand is not to be included in opening bank balances for the purpose of this projection.

Task

Prepare a monthly cash flow forecast for the year ending 30 June 20X6.

Activity 14   Level: MODERATE

This Activity uses the spreadsheet created in Activity 13. The current overdraft facility for Rolling Projections Ltd stands at £50,000. Modify the original spreadsheet so that it shows in which month(s) the facility is likely to be exceeded, and by how much.

Activity 15   Level: MODERATE

You have been selected to work on a special assignment at a subsidiary company. The assignment team will consist of, besides you, the divisional chief accountant, an assistant accountant and a secretary. Because you are familiar with spreadsheets, you have been asked to set up a spreadsheet to record the time which each of you spends on this assignment and to cost it using your group's internal chargeout rates, which are as follows.

	£
Divisional chief accountant	72.50
Assistant accountant	38.00
Accounting technician	21.45
Secretary	17.30

13

Tasks

(a) Design a spreadsheet which will show hours spent and cost per person by week for a three week assignment.

(b) Complete the spreadsheet by entering the following time data, and calculate the total personnel costs of the job.

	Week 3	Week 2	Week 1
You	37 hrs 30 mins	40 hrs	32 hrs
Assistant Accountant	35 hrs	40 hrs	20 hrs
Divisional chief accountant	6 hrs 45 mins	4 hrs 30 mins	-
Secretary	37 hrs 15 mins	32 hrs 10 mins	15 hrs

Activity 16   Level: ADVANCED

This Activity uses the spreadsheet created in Activity 15.

A week later, back at head office, you receive a memo from the divisional chief accountant. He tells you that he has spent a further six hours on the assignment, in week 4. He also wants you to add in to your calculations the costs of two laptop computers which were charged out at £100 per week each for the duration of the three weeks of fieldwork. You have also found out that secretarial chargeout rates were increased by 10% from week 3 onwards.

Task

Update the spreadsheet which you created in Activity 15.

Activity 17   Level: ADVANCED

Although some of the systems in Bright Ideas Ltd, the company you work for, have been computerised, petty cash is still accounted for in a two column cash book. You have decided that this is not very informative and you are about to set up an analysed cash book using a spreadsheet. The following information is relevant.

(a) Petty cash receipts arise from occasional sales to customers who arrive at the factory wishing to make small purchases and who cannot be persuaded to pay by cheque or credit card.

(b) Payments out of petty cash are made for postage, stationery, kitchen supplies (such as coffee and biscuits), purchase of gifts to staff and odd sundries such as taxi fares.

(c) At the end of each week, any excess over £250 is banked and any shortfall made up by cashing a cheque.

Task

Design a sample page for the analysed cash book, using formulae where appropriate. You should find that 20 lines are sufficient for a typical week's transactions. Receipts and payments are always to be entered on separate lines. You should ignore VAT.

Activity 18   Level: ADVANCED

This Activity uses the analysed petty cash book which you designed in Activity 17.

During week 37 (week ending 12 September 20X6) the following transactions take place. On the morning of Monday 8 September, there is £230 in the petty cash tin, together with an IOU for £20 signed by the Finance Director and dated the previous Friday.

Day	Ref	Transaction	Amount £
Monday	2388	Cash sale	25.60
	2389	Cash sale	13.55
	4998	Purchase of coffee	12.96
Tuesday	-	FD repayment	20.00
	2390	Cash sale	25.60
	4999	Padded envelopes	3.95
	4000	First class stamps	25.00
Wednesday	2391	Cash sale	4.00
	2392	Cash sale	13.55
	4001	Wedding present – Alison	74.99
Thursday	4002	Taxi fare	8.00
Friday	2393	Cash sale	12.00
	4003	Christian Aid collector	20.00
	4004	Speedpost packages	32.71

Task

Complete the petty cash book for the week. The final entry should show the payment to or receipt from the bank at the end of the week.

Activity 19 Level: ADVANCED

Bodger & Co is a jobbing company. On 1 September 20X5 there was one uncompleted job in the workshop. The job card for this work can be summarised as follows.

Job costing sheet, Job no 487

	£
Costs to date	
Direct materials	1,025
Direct labour (120 hrs)	525
Production overhead (£3 per direct labour hour)	360
	1,910

A new job (job no. 488) was commenced in September. Production costs were as follows.

	£
Direct materials	
Issued to: job no. 487	3,585
job no. 488	5,850
Damaged stock written off from stores	3,450
	12,585

	£
Material transfers	
From job 487 to job 488	1,125
From job 487 to store	1,305

Direct labour	
Job no. 487	445 hrs
Job no. 488	280 hrs

The cost of labour hours in September was £4.50 per hour. Production overheads incurred during the month were £5,700.

BPP PUBLISHING

Practice activities

The jobs were delivered to customers on completion, and invoiced as follows.

	£
Job 487	8,050
Job 488	12,000

Administration and marketing costs, which totalled £4,800 in September, are added to cost of sales at the rate of 20% of production cost.

Task

Using a spreadsheet package, prepare the summarised job cost cards for each job and calculate the profit on each completed job.

Activity 20   Level: ADVANCED

Vincent is drawing up his accounts for the year ended 31 December 20X7. He has extracted the following balances from his general ledger into the .spreadsheet **Ac_20_Q**, which you will find in your BPP data files.

	£
Fixtures and fittings at cost	21,650
Depreciation at 1 January 20X7	12,965
Motor vehicles at cost	37,628
Depreciation at 1 January 20X7	17,490
Stock at 1 January 20X7	34,285
Sales ledger control account	91,440
Provision for doubtful debts	3,409
Cash in hand	361
Bank	14,297
Purchase ledger control account	102,157
Sales	354,291
Purchases	197,981
Wages and salaries	57,980
Rent and rates	31,650
Advertising	12,240
Administrative expenses	31,498
Bank charges	2,133
Bad debts written off	763
Capital	15,000

The following adjustments are required.

   (a) Depreciation of fixtures and fittings at 20% on cost. Fittings with a cost of £1,880 are already fully written down.

   (b) Depreciation of motor vehicles at 25% on cost. All cars are under three years old except for one (cost £7,640), which has a written down value of £1,146.

   (c) Write-off of a specific debtor balance of £2,440. The provision is to be adjusted to 5% of debtors after this write-off.

   (d) Closing stock was valued at £37,238.

   (e) An accrual has to be made for the fourth quarter's rent of £6,750.

   (f) Sales made between Christmas and the New Year and for which invoices were mislaid for a couple of days (and so not posted) amounted to £4,300.

   (g) Vincent wants to put in £10,000 of additional capital to be reflected in 20X7's accounts.

   (h) Advertising costs include a prepayment of £500 per month for January to March 20X8.

   (i) Bank charges of £508 have not been accrued.

Task

Using the information in the file **Ac_20_Q** Prepare an extended trial balance including final amounts for the profit and loss account and balance sheet.

Activity 21   Level: MODERATE

Dittori Sage Ltd has a sales ledger package which does not offer an aged debtors option. You have decided to set up a simple spreadsheet to monitor ageing by region. The report generator facility on the sales ledger has enabled you to export the following information as at 31 May 20X6 into a spreadsheet. The spreadsheet is file **Ac_21_Q** in your BPP data.

Invoices outstanding

Region	Current	1 month	2 month	3 month	4 month	5 month +
Highlands	346.60	567.84	32.17	-	-	54.80
Strathclyde	24,512.05	28,235.50	4,592.50	1,244.80	51.36	942.57
Borders	1,927.77	-	512.88	-	-	-
North West	824.80	14,388.91	2,473.53	-	482.20	79.66
North East	14,377.20	12,850.00	-	3,771.84	1,244.55	-
Midlands	45,388.27	61,337.88	24,001.02	4,288.31	1,391.27	4,331.11
Wales	14,318.91	5,473.53	21.99	4,881.64	512.27	422.50
East Anglia	157.20	943.68	377.40	1,500.87	15.33	247.66
South West	9,528.73	11,983.39	3,771.89	6,228.77	1,008.21	214.51
South East	68,110.78	83,914.54	29,117.96	24,285.10	14,328.90	5,422.50
France	6,422.80	7,451.47	5,897.55	2,103.70	140.50	3,228.76
Other EU	5,433.88	4,991.90	5,012.70	4,223.80	1,022.43	1,984.29
Rest of World	1,822.70	4,529.67	277.50	3,491.34	-	-

Task

Prepare a spreadsheet which will show the above analysis, total debtors by region and the percentage of debt in each category by region and in total.

Activity 22   Level: MODERATE

A project will **cost** £1.5m (all incurred now) but it is expected to bring about net **savings** as follows.

	£
Year 1	271,000
Year 2	226,000
Year 3	249,000
Year 4	275,000
Year 5	265,000
Year 6	300,000
Year 7	177,000
Year 8	205,000
Year 9	223,000
Year 10	231,000

Task

Use a spreadsheet to find the answer to the following questions.

(a) Determine whether the project should be undertaken if the rate of interest paid on a loan of £1.5m is 10%

(b) It is possible that any day the rate of interest may increase to 11%. Should the project be undertaken if this happens?

(c) At what rate of interest would it not matter whether the project went ahead or not?

17

Activity 23   Level: ADVANCED

Open the spreadsheet file **Ac_23_Q** in your BPP data. You will see the following.

	A	B	C
1	2805TN		
2	1704VR		
3	3501OY		
4	9522CI		
5	8022LJ		
6	6865XY		
7	8506TZ		
8	1091UY		
9	7405RP		
10	5823PK		
11	9456RI		
12	3002QJ		
13	2567UO		
14	2805KM		
15	3309QI		
16	9324WU		
17	1675LW		
18	9941AU		
19	2673DO		
20	7833UH		
21	2769KD		
22	7484TS		
23	6433PE		

These are the first few of 1500 rows containing codes for materials used in your business. The numerical part of the code is your company's reference for the material. The alphabetic part refers to the supplier of the material.

Tasks

(a) Sort all 1500 codes into **supplier** order (ie codes ending AA, codes ending AB, codes ending AC, etc). Use formulae. Do not retype any part of the code. Do not spend more than 5 minutes on this part of the task.

(b) Do any of the codes appear more than once in the list? If so which ones? Again, do not spend more than five minutes trying to find out.

Activity 24   Level: ADVANCED

The following illustration shows a spreadsheet model for calculating depreciation of fixed assets on either a straight line basis or a reducing balance basis.

The idea is that the user enters figures in cells F3 to F6 and the model automatically calculates an annual depreciation charge, over up to 10 years.

The user enter the cost of the asset the rate of depreciation, the method of depreciation ("s" for straight line; "r" for reducing balance). If the user wishes, there can also be a materiality level: a fixed asset will be written down to nil in the following year if its carried forward book value is lower than the materiality limit (if there is no limit the user just enters 0 in the Materiality cell).

Task

Devise a model that works like this.

	A	B	C	D	E	F	G	H	I	J	K
1											
2											
3					Cost	4599					
4					Rate	0.35					
5					Method	r					
6					Materiality	500					
7											
8											
9											
10											
11		Year 1	Year 2	Year 3	Year 4	Year 5	Year 6	Year 7	Year 8	Year 9	Year 10
12	NBV b/f	4599.00	2989.35	1943.08	1263.00	820.95	533.62	346.85	0.00	0.00	0.00
13	Depreciation	1609.65	1046.27	680.08	442.05	287.33	186.77	346.85	0.00	0.00	0.00
14	NBV c/f	2989.35	1943.08	1263.00	820.95	533.62	346.85	0.00	0.00	0.00	0.00
15											
16											

Activity 25   Level: ADVANCED

We have included this activity as a recent Simulation tested database skills. This activity requires **Microsoft Access** 97 or above.

Situation

An ex-accountant set up a PC support helpline under the trading name PC Plod. PC Plod now has four part time employees and a good reputation for solving PC related problems. Customers phone the PC Plod helpline to receive assistance.

The charge for each call is dependent on the length of the call and the product supported. Details of each call are entered into an Access database. The database is available within your BPP data in the C:\BPPU21\Access directory. Open the file **PC Plod.mdb** now.

Tasks

(a) Ensure the Tables tab is active and from the menu at the top of the screen select **Tools, Relationships**. Now use the menu at the top of the screen to select **Relationships, Show Table**. Individually highlight and **Add** the Calls, Product Classification and Rates tables to the view. Close the Show Table window. The Relationships window will now look like this.

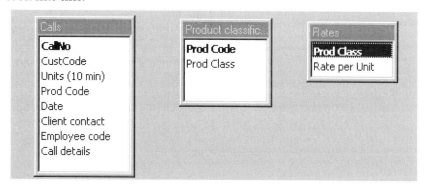

BPP PUBLISHING

(b) Click and **hold down** the mouse over *Prod Code* within Calls, **drag** the pointer over to *Prod Code* within Product classification and **release** the mouse button. Click **Create** within the pop-up window. Repeat the process for *Prod Class* within Product classification and *Prod Class* within Rates. The Relationships window will now show the relationships you have established (see below). **Close** the Relationships window (use **File, Close** or the × symbol in the top right corner of the window) and click **Yes** to save your changes.

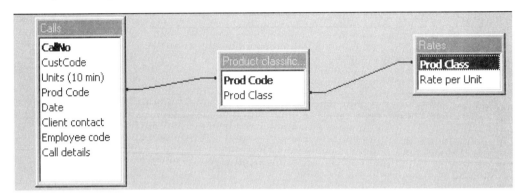

(c) Activate the **Queries** tab, click on **New,** highlight **Simple Query Wizard** and click **OK.**

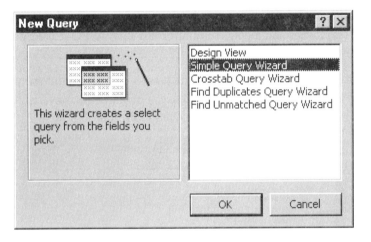

(d) Ensure the Calls table is displayed in the Tables/Queries box. Individually highlight and select the fields *CallNo, CustCode, Units (10 min)* and *Prod Code* using the ⟩ button. The selection window should now look like this.

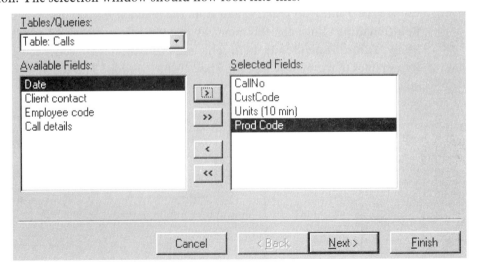

(e) Use the 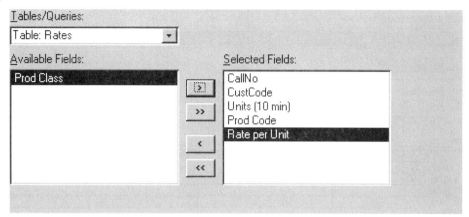 button to change the table selected within the Tables/Queries box to Rates. Add *Rate per Unit* to the Selected Fields. Your selection should look like the picture below. Click **Next.**

(f) You will then be presented with the option of Summary or Detail level. Accept the default of **Detail** by clicking **Next.**

(g) You will be asked to give the Query a meaningful name. Call this query 'Call charge to customer'. Accept the default selection of **Open** the query to view information by clicking **Finish**.

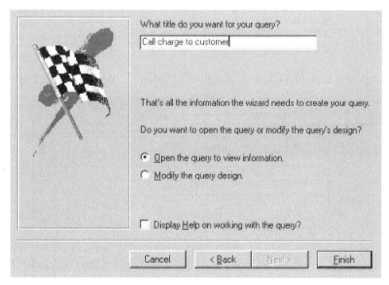

The Query will run automatically, leaving the resulting data sheet open, as shown in the sample below.

Call Number	CustCode	Units (10 min)	Prod Code	Rate per Unit
1	JONESA	3	WIN98	£10.00
2	WILLIB	2	SAGE	£10.00
4	JOHNST	1	EXCEL	£10.00
5	SPOONE	2	ACCESS	£10.00
7	BERRYA	4	WORD	£10.00
8	HEMIB	6	ACCESS	£10.00
10	FOWLER	5	WIN98	£10.00
11	OWENM	8	PRINTER	£10.00

Call charge to customer : Select Query

(h) We will modify this Query to calculate the amount to be charged out for each call. Close the datasheet. (Use **File, Close** or the × symbol in the top right corner of the window.) The new query will be highlighted. Click the **Design** button. The active window should now look like the picture below.

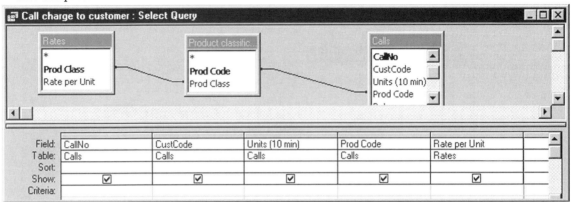

(i) Click in the blank Field box to the right of *Rate per Unit*. Rather than selecting an existing field (which can be picked from a list obtained by clicking the down arrow) we are going to write an **Expression** to calculate the charge out amount for each call. **Type the text shown below into the box.** You must type this **exactly** as shown. Note the use of square brackets - this tells Access that we are using the name of an existing field.

Charge to Customer: [Units (10 min)]*[Rate per Unit]

This Expression will multiply *Units* by the *Rate per Unit*, and call the result *Charge to Customer*.

Click the small **Show** box and **Close** the current window, **saving** your changes.

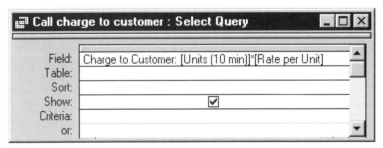

(j) If you run the Query now (either double click the Query name or click **Open** while the Query is highlighted) the resulting data sheet will include the calculated *Charge to Customer*. (Sample shown below.)

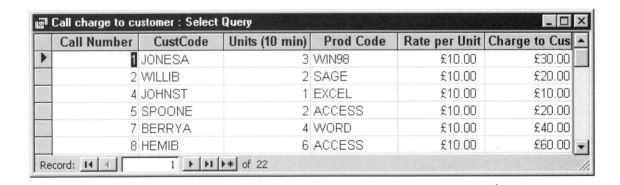

(k) Close the data sheet. It would be useful to have the name of the PC Plod employee who dealt with the call included in this query. The employee code is held within the Calls table, but the full employee name (*Solution Provider*) is held only in the Employees table.

Click on **Design** then from the menu options at the top of the screen select **Query, Show table** and **Add** the Employees table. **Close** the Show Table window.

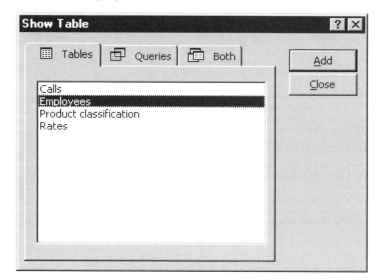

(l) The Query design window wil now be active. If Access has not automatically recognised the Relationship between the Calls and Employees tables, follow the procedure explained in (b) to establish the Relationship using the common field (*Employee code*).

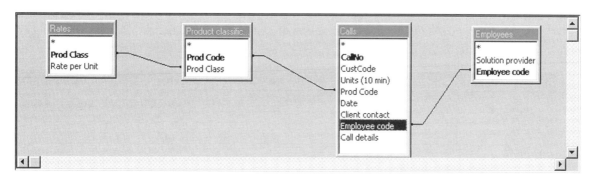

(m) Click on *Solution provider* within the Employees table, hold the mouse button down and drag Solution provider into the blank Field box to the right of *Charge to Customer*. (Double clicking *Solution provider* within the Employees table would achieve the same outcome.) Close the Query design window, saving your changes.

CallNc	CustCoc	Units (10	Prod Co	Rate per	Charge to Custo	Solution provider
Calls	Calls	Calls	Calls	Rates		Employees
☑	☑	☑	☑	☑	☑	☑

(n)   Run the Query to see the data sheet with *Solution provider* added. (Sample shown below.)

Call Nu	Date	CustCode	Units	Prod Code	Rate per Uni	Charge to C	Solution provider
1	01/06/99	JONESA	3	WIN98	£10.00	£30.00	Julie Rogers
2	01/06/99	WILLIB	2	SAGE	£10.00	£20.00	David Jones
4	01/06/99	JOHNST	1	EXCEL	£10.00	£10.00	Natalie Spooner
5	01/06/99	SPOONE	2	ACCESS	£10.00	£20.00	Julie Rogers
7	01/06/99	BERRYA	4	WORD	£10.00	£40.00	Frank Wilson
8	01/06/99	HEMIB	6	ACCESS	£10.00	£60.00	Julie Rogers

(o)   Copy the Query. (Highlight the Query, select **Edit, Copy** and then **Edit, Paste** from the menu at the top of the screen. Call the copied query *Trial and Error*.)

(p)   Change the design of the query *Trial and Error* as indicated below. (Run the query and examine the results after each change.)

- Within Query Design click in the Sort box of *Prod Code* and sort records in ascending order.

- Remove the *Prod Code* sort and sort records based on the *Charge to Customer* – in descending order.

- Add the field *Client contact* (from the Calls table) to the Query.

- Experiment any way you like with the Query design options.

(q)   We wish to export to Excel the data extracted using the Query *Call charge to customer*, but only for calls taken 01/06/99 to 02/06/99. Use the skills you have gained to add the *Date* field to the *Call charge to customer* query, and restrict the records extracted by entering 'Between 01/06/99 And 02/06/99' in the Criteria box of *Date*. (As shown below – Access will insert the # at each end of the dates.) Close the design window and **Save** your changes.

Call charge to customer : Select Query

Field:	CallNo	Date		CustCode	Units (10 n	Prod Coc	Rate per l	Charge tc	Solution provic
Table:	Calls	Calls		Calls	Calls	Calls	Rates		Employees
Sort:									
Show:	☑	☑		☑	☑	☑	☑	☑	☑
Criteria:		Between #01/06/99# And #02/06/99#							

Follow the steps outlined below to **export data from Access to Excel**.

Step 1.   Ensure the Query or Table you wish to export is highlighted. (We will use the Query produced in (q)). From the menu at the top of the screen select **File, Save As/Export... .**

Step 2.   Accept the default of **To an external file or database** by clicking **OK.**

Step 3.   Choose the location (in the **Save in** box) and enter 'Calls 01/06/99 to 02/06/99' in the **File name** box. The remaining box on the active window is the **Save as type** box. Click the down arrow and select your version of **Microsoft Excel.** (e.g. Excel 4 or Excel 97)

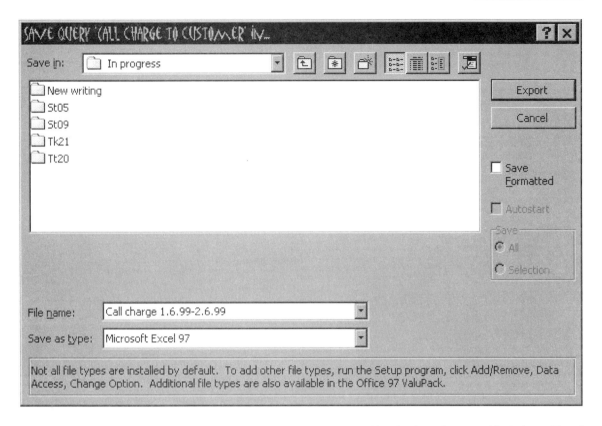

Step 4. Click **Export**. The spreadsheet will be created in the location specified. Start Excel and open the spreadsheet to see the exported data.

Note: Depending on how Microsoft Office was installed, it is possible that within ***Step3,*** the **Save as type** box will not give Excel as an option. An **alternative method** is, after highlighting the Query or Table to export, select **Tools** from the pull down menu, then **Office Links, Analyse it with MS Excel.** Excel will then show your toolbar at the bottom of the screen – click on this and you will see the spreadsheet data.

(r)   Within Excel select **Data, Sort.** Sort the data by *Solution provider* in Ascending order.

(s)   From Excel's menu select **Data, Subtotal** and select the criteria shown below.

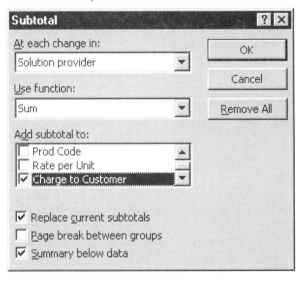

This report would provide useful daily summary of revenue generated. The date range can easily be amended within the Query. You may like to add a heading and use Excel's formatting functions to tidy up the 'Calls 01/06/99 to 02/06/99' spreadsheet you have created.

BPP PUBLISHING

Practice
Devolved
Assessments

Practice devolved assessment
1 *Broom Riggs*

Performance criteria

The following performance criteria are covered in this Devolved Assessment.

Element 21.1

Obtain information from a computerised Management Information System

1	The required information is correctly located within the MIS structure
2	Advice is sought where there are difficulties in obtaining the required information
4	Information is checked for its accuracy and completeness
5	Information is stored in a format which helps others to access it and use it

Element 21.2

Produce spreadsheets for the analysis of numerical information

1	The spreadsheet is titled in a way which clearly defines its use and purpose
2	The arrangement of the spreadsheet is consistent with organisational conventions
3	All rates and other numeric inputs and assumptions are stated to the correct number of decimal places
4	Calculated values are checked for correctness when changes are made to the inputs
5	The spreadsheet is used to carry out data modifications and for entry of related formulas
6	Each cell is formatted clearly and accurately
7	A method is selected to eliminate rounding errors which is suitable for the purpose of the spreadsheet

Notes on completing this Devolved Assessment

This Devolved Assessment is designed to test your ability to use a Management Information System.

You are provided with information to complete tasks (a) to (j).

You are allowed 2 hours to complete your work

A high level of accuracy is required. Check your work carefully.

Correcting fluid should not be used. Errors should be crossed out neatly and clearly. You should write in ink - not in pencil.

BPP
PUBLISHING

Note to tutors

Tasks (a), (d), (e) (f) and (i) require access to the computer's hard disk and/or file management facilities. If access or facilities are restricted on your system these tasks may need to be modified.

PRACTICE DEVOLVED ASSESSMENT 1: BROOM RIGGS

Data

Broom Riggs Ltd is a company engaged in the sale of watersports equipment and accessories. It was established in 20X1 and operates from leasehold retail premises. Although its customer base consists mainly of individual callers, it does also supply some goods to trade customers, for example, a local water-ski club and two sailing clubs.

The company is now preparing accounts for the year ended 31 December 20X8. The trial balance as at 31 December 20X8 is as follows. This is available in the file **DA1_Q** in the BPP data.

Folio	Account	DR £	CR £
A1	Accountancy fees	440.00	
A2	Advertising	1,556.29	
B1	Bank account		27,488.12
B2	Bank charges	2,157.51	
B3	Bank interest	1,109.11	
B4	Bad debt expense		
C1	Credit card charges	2,212.80	
D1	Discounts allowed	5,629.31	
D2	Discounts received		4,529.69
D3	Directors' loan accounts	9,343.89	
D4	Depreciation (accumulated)		
	Fixtures and fittings		14,304.00
	Motor vehicles		22,563.10
	Leasehold		38,500.00
D5	Depreciation expense		
D6	Doubtful debt provision		
E1	Electricity	7,264.61	
F1	Fixtures and fittings	35,430.00	
G1	Gas	12,374.97	
I1	Insurance	22,298.96	
L1	Leasehold	220,000.00	
L2	Loan		50,000.00
L3	Loan interest	5,000.00	
M1	Maintenance	4,649.22	
M2	Motor expenses	1,557.10	
M3	Motor vehicles	73,482.10	
P1	Profit and loss account		160,808.95
P2	Purchases	499,227.91	
P3	Purchase ledger control account		51,444.74
P4	Petty cash	1,000.00	
P5	Purchase returns		687.08
P6	Print, post and stationery	5,885.32	
P7	PAYE and NI	91,799.27	
R1	Rates	30,616.08	
R2	Rent (warehouse)	18,125.00	
S1	Share capital		100,000.00
S2	Sales		1,022,734.87
S3	Sales ledger control account	105,947.07	
S4	Sales returns	2,287.03	
S5	Staff welfare	1,768.56	

S6	Stock at 1 January 20X8	48,172.29	
S7	Sundry expenses	1,574.68	
T1	Telephone	8,763.82	
V1	VAT		18,965.89
W1	Wages and salaries	266,449.27	
W2	Water rates	9,454.27	
X1	Suspense account	16,450.00	

The following transactions and adjustments must be taken into account in the preparation of the trial balance.

(a) Fixed asset adjustments required are as follows.

 (i) The lease, which has a 40 year term, was purchased on 1 January 20X1. Depreciation, which is to be calculated on a straight line basis, has not yet been provided for the year ended 31 December 20X8.

 (ii) Depreciation has not yet been provided on the motor vehicles, which are depreciated at 25% on written down value.

 (iii) Depreciation is also still to be provided on fixtures and fittings at 10% of cost. A full year of depreciation is charged in the year of acquisition.

(b) The suspense account comprises the following items.

 (i) A new piece of fixed asset furniture was purchased during the year for £12,250.00 for cash but it was posted to the suspense account as it had not been classified.

 (ii) The company had paid £4,000 in cash for maintenance work but the bookkeeper had been unsure about whether to treat it as a capital or revenue item and it had been posted to the suspense account. The entire amount relates to revenue expenditure.

 (iii) The cash paid near the year end for the staff Christmas party (£450.00) had been posted to the suspense account

 (iv) One of the directors put an expenses claim in for £250.00 at the end of the year and this has been posted to the suspense account rather than the director's loan account. The relevant expense accounts have already been adjusted.

(c) Bank charges to be posted are as follows.

 (i) A bank statement received at the end of January showed that bank charges of £522.18 had been incurred for the three months ended 31 January 20X9.

 (ii) The last time bank interest was charged was 31 October 20X8. The average overdrawn balance in November and December was £22,000. The prevailing average interest rate was 12% per annum.

(d) Stock related items are as follows.

 (i) On 2 January 20X9, goods with a cost of £511.42, which had been purchased by the company before the year end on credit, were returned to suppliers. The goods had been omitted from the year-end stock valuation.

 (ii) Goods sold for £2,117.28 were returned by customers just after the year end. The stock has been included in the year end stock figure at cost, but no other adjustment has been made.

 (iii) The closing stock was counted and valued at £67,329.53

(e) It has been discovered after the year end that a trade debtor owing £2,200.00 has gone into liquidation and there is no prospect of recovering any of the money. It has also been decided that, for the first time, a general provision should be made for doubtful debts. This is to be calculated as ½% of net trade debtors.

(f)   Other matters are as follows.

  (i)   An insurance bill was paid on 1 April 20X8 for £18,178.44 for the year to 31 March 20X9

  (ii)   The audit fee of £3,000.00 must be accrued under accountancy fees.

  (iii)   On 29 December 20X8 the company paid £3,625.00 rent for the quarter to 25 March 20X9.

  (iv)   The Uniform Business Rate paid on 1 April 19X8 for 12 months was £24,492.88

  (v)   The water rates bill paid on 1 April 19X8 for 12 months was £7,954.28.

Tasks

(a)   Set up a spreadsheet which will be used to prepare an extended trial balance. Enter the opening trial balance as at 31 December 20X8 and ensure that it balances. Save it on the computer's hard disk.

(b)   Print out the opening trial balance including the folio references, account names, debits and credits.

(c)   Obtain a floppy disk and check that it is free from viruses.

(d)   Create a subdirectory called BROOM on the floppy disk and save the trial balance in this subdirectory. If not, save the TB as a file named BROOM in the A:\directory.

(e)   Delete your trial balance from the hard disk and, once you have closed down the spreadsheet application and any other open applications, switch off your computer and any related peripheral devices.

(f)   Switch the computer back on and *copy* your spreadsheet file back onto the hard disk.

(g)   Set the floppy disk to write protect and place it in a suitable storage container

(h)   Returning to your spreadsheet, make the adjustments required to the trial balance and complete the extended trial balance. Document any calculations you make either on paper or on the spreadsheet, and submit these with your work.

(i)   Save the completed ETB (as, say, BROOM1) on the floppy disk you used earlier. Do *not* overwrite any files already on the floppy disk.

(j)   Print out on a single sheet of paper the complete spreadsheet containing the ETB.

Practice devolved assessment
2   *Wild Thyme*

Performance criteria

The following performance criteria are covered in this Devolved Assessment.

Element 21.1

Obtain information from a computerised Management Information System

1   The required information is correctly located within the MIS structure

2   Advice is sought where there are difficulties in obtaining the required information

3   Additional authorisation is obtained for sensitive or confidential information in accordance with the organisation's security regulations

4   Information is checked for its accuracy and completeness

5   Information is stored in a format which helps others to access it and use it

6   Confidential information is kept secure and not disclosed to unauthorised people

Element 21.2

Produce spreadsheets for the analysis of numerical information

1   The spreadsheet is titled in a way which clearly defines its use and purpose

2   The arrangement of the spreadsheet is consistent with organisational conventions

3   All rates and other numeric inputs and assumptions are stated to the correct number of decimal places

4   Calculated values are checked for correctness when changes are made to the inputs

5   The spreadsheet is used to carry out data modifications and for entry of related formulas

6   Each cell is formatted clearly and accurately

7   A method is selected to eliminate rounding errors which is suitable for the purpose of the spreadsheet

8   Confidential information is kept secure and not disclosed to unauthorised people

Element 21.3

Contribute to the quality of the Management Information System

2   Suggestions for changes are supported by a clear rationale as to how they could improve the quality of the system

3   The reliability of assumptions and judgements made is assessed and clearly stated

5   Suggestions are presented clearly and in a way which helps people to understand and act on them

Notes on completing this Devolved Assessment

This Devolved Assessment is designed to test your ability to use a Management Information System.

You are provided with information to complete tasks (a) to (k).

You are allowed 2 hours to complete your work

A high level of accuracy is required. Check your work carefully.

Correcting fluid should not be used. Errors should be crossed out neatly and clearly. You should write in ink - not in pencil.

PRACTICE DEVOLVED ASSESSMENT 2: WILD THYME

Data

Wild Thyme Ltd is a company which makes tents. It has three production departments and two service departments.

The cutting and sewing department occupies 3,000 square metres of floor space, the framemaking department 1,750 square metres and the assembly operation, which deals with such matters as stitching on of zips and guy ropes, 1,500 square metres.

The maintenance department occupies 800 square metres and the staff restaurant is in a 600 square metre area. Budgeted rent and rates costs for 20X7 are £8.20 per square metre for the whole of the site.

Other details relating to these departments are set out below. All figures are budgeted for the coming year, 20X7. These details are not available on file.

Departmental statistics	*C*	*F*	*A*	*M*	*R*
Plant value (£'000)	32	20	16	8	4
Hourly labour rate	£4.10	£5.14	£4.25	£4.00	£3.20
Direct labour hours	4,200	1,200	2,000		

Allocated overheads	*C*	*F*	*A*	*M*	*R*
Specific to each department (£'000)	4.8	2.2	3.5	2.0	1.6
Maintenance	20%	58%	22%		
Restaurant	55%	18%	27%		

Rent and rates costs are to be apportioned on the basis of floor area. Other budgeted costs, and the relevant basis of apportionment for each, are set out below

Overhead	*Total*	*Basis of apportionment*
	£	
Machine insurance	8,350	Plant value
Depreciation	16,450	Plant value
Production supervisor	24,300	Direct labour hours
Heat and light	8,800	Floor area

Tasks

(a)   Prepare a spreadsheet showing the overhead cost budgeted for each department.

(b)   Make two copies of the spreadsheet on a spare floppy disk.

(c)   The budgeted figures for the coming year are still confidential. Write a short note explaining what steps and precautions you would take if you wished to send the floppy disk you have just used to a colleague in your organisation, using internal mail.

(d)   If you can, delete one copy of the spreadsheet which you saved on the floppy disk.

(e)   Write a short note explaining what steps you would take to recover a deleted file. (Assume that you do not still have a copy on the PC.)

(f)   Using the data provided, calculate overhead absorption rates for each department based on direct labour hours.

(g)   Improve the presentation of your spreadsheet (including the data table prepared in part (a)) so that it is suitable for inclusion in a management report.

(h)   Print out a copy of the final spreadsheet on a single sheet of paper.

(i)   Make a new back-up copy of the spreadsheet on your floppy disk.

(j)   You learn that the budget, which has now been agreed, includes two amendments. The production supervisor's costs will be £25,200 and heat and light are expected to cost £9,500. Revise your spreadsheet accordingly.

(k)   Close down all open applications and switch off your equipment.

Practice devolved assessment
3   *Island Quay*

Performance criteria

The following performance criteria are covered in this Devolved Assessment.

Element 21.1

Obtain information from a computerised Management Information System

1   The required information is correctly located within the MIS structure

2   Advice is sought where there are difficulties in obtaining the required information

4   Information is checked for its accuracy and completeness

5   Information is stored in a format which helps others to access it and use it

Element 21.2

Produce spreadsheets for the analysis of numerical information

1   The spreadsheet is titled in a way which clearly defines its use and purpose

2   The arrangement of the spreadsheet is consistent with organisational conventions

3   All rates and other numeric inputs and assumptions are stated to the correct number of decimal places

4   Calculated values are checked for correctness when changes are made to the inputs

5   The spreadsheet is used to carry out data modifications and for entry of related formulas

6   Each cell is formatted clearly and accurately

7   A method is selected to eliminate rounding errors which is suitable for the purpose of the spreadsheet

Notes on completing this Devolved Assessment

This Devolved Assessment is designed to test your ability to use a management information system.

You are provided with information to complete tasks (a) to (e).

You are allowed 3 hours to complete your work.

A high level of accuracy is required. Check your work carefully.

Correcting fluid should not be used. Errors should be crossed out neatly and clearly. You should write in ink - not in pencil

BPP
PUBLISHING

PRACTICE DEVOLVED ASSESSMENT: ISLAND QUAY

Data

Your company, Island Quay plc, is in the process of setting up a customer services department. Your supervisor is the Chief Accountant (Customer Services). She is keen to set up an accurate system of performance reporting for the department. The department will not, in the short term at least, generate any income of its own and the main board wishes to examine its performance carefully following an initial investment of £180,000, which represents the department's capital, before either committing further funding at a later date or re-allocating sales revenues to the department.

The department receives sales data from the sales order processing department and, acting on this, processes and issues warranty documentation whenever a warranty sale is made. A record is kept of the number of warranties issued as a measure of output. When a customer requires a warranty repair (following initial investigation by telephone), he or she completes a warranty claim form included in the documentation and posts or faxes it to the department setting out details of the problem or breakdown encountered.

When a warranty claim is received (on average one year into the life of the warranty), a repair is carried out. The number of repairs is also seen as a measure of output.

The department will also have responsibility for carrying out a component testing programme and for performing a limited amount of additional research.

Resources used by the department comprise labour, other running costs (including cost of spare parts and consumables) and the cost of capital. Resources used are to be attributed to the department's activities in the following ratios initially.

Issuing warranties	5%
Warranty repairs	60%
Testing	25%
Research	10%

Tasks

Your supervisor, who has a public sector background, has devised a format for performance reporting. She has left you a set of notes and left the office for a week's management training course in the Brecon Beacons. She expects your work to be completed before her return.

(a) Design a spreadsheet which could be used to report the required variables over a four year period. Include suitable sub-headings rather than simply listing all the variables in one group.

(b) Insert the relevant data from your supervisor's notes and complete the spreadsheet. You will need to refer to your own notes of telephone calls as well in order to complete this task.

(c) Save the spreadsheet and close down all applications.

(d) Open the spreadsheet again. Write a brief note describing what you would do if, on trying to open the file, you received a message which said 'Error. Unable to open file.'

(e) Print out a copy of the final spreadsheet on a single sheet of paper. Use appropriate formatting functions to improve its appearance.

Inter-office memo

To: Accounting Technician
From: Chief Accountant (Customer Services)

Can you have the performance report ready for me to take into the divisional board meeting on my return? We need to include the following items.

1   *Inflation*. Use general price deflator, with Year 1 as base, as follows.

Year 1:	1.00
Year 2:	1.04
Year 3:	1.08
Year 4:	1.13
Year 5:	1.19

2   *Value of capital*. We need to depreciate the department's capital over five years, on a straight line basis, and adjust the depreciated value for inflation. (Eg, value of capital in year 2 is £180,000 × 0.8 × 1.04 and in year 3 it is £180,000 × 0.6 × 1.08.)

3   *Annual capital charge*. This is the amount of depreciation (inflated) plus an allowance for the cost of capital, calculated as 7% of the mid-year value. So in year one the charge is £47,542. (This is calculated as $£180,000 \times 0.2 + \dfrac{£180,000 + £149,760}{2} \times 7\%$.)

4   *'Physical' capital consumed*. Annual capital charge deflated by general price deflator.

5   *Hours worked*. Check with customer services director.

6   *Labour costs*. £205,000 in year 1, £200,000 in year 2 and rising by 2% in each subsequent year.

7   *Average wage rate*. This must be shown.

8   *Other running costs*. Check with finance director.

9   *'Physical' other running costs*. This is other running costs deflated.

10 *Total annual cost*. Put in a total which adds annual capital charge (3), labour costs (6) and other running costs (8).

11 *Total 'physical' running costs*. Add 'physical' other running costs and physical labour (obtained from hours worked weighted by the base year unit cost, ie hours worked multiplied by the Year 1 average wage rate).

12 *Total' physical' resources consumed*. This is total 'physical' running costs and 'physical' capital consumed.

13 *Warranties issued*. Check with customer services manager.

14 *Repairs performed*. Check with customer services manager.

15 *Total costs: issuing warranties*. Take relevant percentage of total annual cost.

BPP PUBLISHING

16   *Unit cost: issuing warranties.* Must be shown.

17   *Real unit cost of issuing warranties.* Divide unit cost by general price deflator

18   *Total costs: performing repairs.* See (15).

19   *Unit cost: performing repairs.* As above. Assume £250 in Year 1. Remember that repairs are a year later than warranty issues, so take previous year cost from (18), inflate by cost of capital and by general price deflator relative to the previous year, then divide by current year output.

20   *Real unit cost of performing repairs.* As for warranties (see above).

21   *'Physical' output of warranties and repairs.* This is the sum of the outputs weighted by their respective base year (Year 1) unit costs, so in Year 1 we take 6400 × unit cost of issuing warranty + 620 × £250.

22   *'Physical' running costs: warranties and repairs.* Take relevant percentage of Total 'physical' running costs.

23   *Productivity of running costs: warranties and repairs.* This is calculated from the previous two lines and is obtained by dividing 'physical' output by 'physical' running costs.

24   *Year-on-year increase in (23).* Put this in as a percentage.

25   *Total 'physical' resources consumed: warranties and repairs.* Calculated on same basis as (22).

26   *Productivity of all resources: warranties and repairs.* Divide previous line into 'physical' output of warranties and repairs.

27   *Year-on- year increase in (26).* Show as percentage.

Note of telephone call.

Customer services director.

Hours worked in department: 30,000 per annum.

Note of telephone call.

Finance director's PA

Other running costs are as follows:

£62,000 in year 1, then £2,000 increase in each of next 2 years and £64,000 in year 4.

Note of telephone call.

Customer Services Manager

Year	Warranties	Repairs
1	6,400	620
2	6,800	700
3	6,800	640
4	7,000	660

BPP
PUBLISHING

Practice devolved assessment
4 York Town

Performance criteria

The following performance criteria are covered in this Devolved Assessment.

Element 21.1

Obtain information from a computerised Management Information System

1   The required information is correctly located within the MIS structure

4   Information is checked for its accuracy and completeness

5   Information is stored in a format which helps others to access it and use it

Element 21.2

Produce spreadsheets for the analysis of numerical information

1   The spreadsheet is titled in a way which clearly defines its use and purpose

2   The arrangement of the spreadsheet is consistent with organisational conventions

3   All rates and other numeric inputs and assumptions are stated to the correct number of decimal places

4   Calculated values are checked for correctness when changes are made to the inputs

5   The spreadsheet is used to carry out data modifications and for entry of related formulas

6   Each cell is formatted clearly and accurately

7   A method is selected to eliminate rounding errors which is suitable for the purpose of the spreadsheet

Element 21.3

Contribute to the quality of the Management Information System

1   Potential improvements to the MIS are identified and considered for their impact on the quality of the system and any interrelated systems

2   Suggestions for changes are supported by a clear rationale as to how they could improve the qualityof the system

3   The reliability of assumptions and judgements made is assessed and clearly stated

4   The benefits and costs of all changes are described accurately

5   Suggestions are presented clearly and in a way which helps people to understand and act on them

45

Notes on completing this Devolved Assessment

This Devolved Assessment is designed to test your ability to use a Management Information System.

You are provided with information to complete tasks (a) to (f).

You are allowed 3 hours to complete your work

A high level of accuracy is required. Check your work carefully.

Correcting fluid should not be used. Errors should be crossed out neatly and clearly. You should write in ink - not in pencil.

Note to tutors

Tasks (a) to (f) require access to the computer's hard disk and/or file management facilities.

Background information

York Town Electrical Ltd is a retail shop selling electronic goods to the general public. It's product range includes computers, CD players, etc with some accessories for these items. You have recently been employed as an assistant to the Financial Accountant. Your main duties include the production of financial reports and other projects for the Financial Accountant.

It is now early July 2000. The Financial Accountant is unhappy with the stock summary produced by stores showing year-end stock information (the year end was June 30). You have been asked to produce a report for the Financial Accountant which will provide some analysis of the stock information, as well as noting any weaknesses in the stock file provided to the accountant.

Tasks

(a)   Load the spreadsheet filename **DA4_Q** and save it with a name of your own choosing.

(b)   Check the accuracy of total cost column. Calculate the total difference found.

(c)   Calculate

- Total stock cost

- Stock ageing by month (take last moved date - year end date to give number of days since stock last moved)

- Stock provision less 90 days = 0%, 90 to 180 = 25% and so on). Make full provision for certain lines

(d)   Find

- Items with high stock levels (more than say 100) which have not moved in the last three months for additional provision

(e)   Further analysis

- Extract stock lines relating to computers only and copy to separate sheet

- Comment briefly on the suitability of the computers for sale and the inadequacy of the stock provision for computers

(f)   Produce a report for the Financial Accountant

- Summarising the above information highlighting any weaknesses in the client stock valuation system and noting how the quality of the information from the stock system should be improved

- Including a bar chart showing aged value of stock lines, and

- Showing the ten highest value items and calculated percentage of total value in these items

Trial Run
Devolved
Assessments

Trial run devolved assessment
5 Marvels Ltd

Performance criteria

The following performance criteria are covered in this Devolved Assessment.

Element 21.1
Obtain information from a computerised Management Information System

1   The required information is correctly located within the MIS structure

2   Advice is sought where there are difficulties in obtaining the required information

3   Additional authorisation is obtained for sensitive or confidential information in accordance with the organisation's security regulations

4   Information is checked for its accuracy and completeness

5   Information is stored in a format which helps others to access it and use it

6   Confidential information is kept secure and not disclosed to unauthorised people

Element 21.2
Produce spreadsheets for the analysis of numerical information

1   The spreadsheet is titled in a way which clearly defines its use and purpose

2   The arrangement of the spreadsheet is consistent with organisational conventions

3   All rates and other numeric inputs and assumptions are stated to the correct number of decimal places

4   Calculated values are checked for correctness when changes are made to the inputs

5   The spreadsheet is used to carry out data modifications and for entry of related formulas

6   Each cell is formatted clearly and accurately

7   A method is selected to eliminate rounding errors which is suitable for the purpose of the spreadsheet

8   Confidential information is kept secure and not disclosed to unauthorised people

Element 21.3
Contribute to the quality of the Management Information System

1   Potential improvements to the MIS are identified and considered for their impact on the quality of the system and any interrelated systems

2   Suggestions for changes are supported by a clear rationale as to how they could improve the quality of the system

3   The reliability of assumptions and judgements made is assessed and clearly stated

4   The benefits and costs of all changes are described accurately

5   Suggestions are presented clearly and in a way which helps people to understand and act on them

Notes on completing the Simulation

This simulation is designed to test your ability to use a management information system.

The situation and tasks are set out for you on pages **53** to **55.**

You are allowed **4 hours** to complete your work.

A high level of accuracy is required. Check your work carefully.

Any spreadsheet that you create should be in good form with proper formatting and making use of a full range of facilities offered. You will not be penalised if the hardware and software tht you use are not the very latest versions. It will not count against you if, for example, you do not have a colour printer or your package does not contain multiple pages.

Attention should be paid to the presentation of your output and reports. You should make full use of the printing facilties, for exmple to make sure that you include proper titles and include headers and footers where appropriate.

Any computer files that are presented for assessment should be on a floppy disk that is clearly marked with your name, the fact that the disk is part of an AAT simulation and the name of the responsible tutor. You should also list the names of the the files on the disk. Filenames should give some indication of their content.

You may either present your answers to the written tasks in handwritten form or as a word processed document if you wish. If you hand write, correcting fluid may be used but it should be used in moderation. Errors should be crossed out neatly and clearly. You should write in black ink, not pencil.

You are advised to read the whole simulation before commencing as all information may be of value and is not necessarly supplied in the sequence in which you would wish to deal with it.

A full solution to this Assessment is provided on page 117 and in the BPP file supplied with this book. Do not turn to the suggested solution until you have completed all parts of the Assessment. Do not open the spreadsheet file containing the solution until until you have completed all parts of the Assessment.

TRIAL RUN DEVOLVED ASSESSMENT: MARVELS LTD

The situation

Introduction

Marvels Ltd is a manufacturing company which started up just over a year ago. The company makes small but ingenious gadgets for the DIY market, invented by Charles Davis, who is the Managing Director of the company. Business was slow to begin with, but sales have rocketed since one of the company's products was featured in a popular television programme on home improvements.

Marvels Ltd now has over 400 customers including major DIY stores in many of the larger cities in the UK (the company is based in London). Repeat orders are regular because the gadget lasts for about three months before it is worn out and has to be replaced.

At present the company's success is making it difficult to meet demand, and it has grown so quickly that administrative matters have been neglected. Expansion plans are under way, including new premises and a number of new staff, of which you, a qualified accountant, are the first to be appointed.

The accounting records

In the opening months of business records were kept using a manual system. These records have gradually been transferred onto spreadsheets representing the major areas of the business (purchases, sales, cash etc). However, the system has become difficult to maintain and there are frequently discrepancies between one set of figures and another.

The sales ledger, for instance, shows name, address and telephone number information, and analyses debts outstanding by age. Debts older than 90 days are written off. There have been very few write-offs to date.

Here are selected rows and columns from the spreadsheet to give you an idea of what you will find (note, some columns are hidden in this illustration for reasons of space).

	A	B	E	F	K	L	M
1					31-60	61-90	Total
2	Fads	Putney High Street	London	SW15 1SP	246.97	62.62	577.15
3	B & Q DIY Supercentre	Blythwood Industrial Estate	Renfrew	PA4 9EU	1087.00	168.24	2885.75
4	D I Y Woodstock	111 A Neilston Road	Paisley	PA2 6ER	524.37	15.92	1326.85
5	D T S	Chester Road East	Deeside	CH5 1QD	537.66	66.60	1261.40
6	Tuck & Norris Ltd	622 Lordship Lane	London	N22 5JH	756.18	72.50	1332.80
7	Cardiff Paint Supplies	51-53 Carlisle Street	Cardiff	CF2 2DR	641.98	117.27	1243.55
8	Great Mills D I Y	Beardmore Park	Ipswich	IP5 7RX	688.37	12.08	1219.75
9	Do-it-yourself	82 Niddrie Road	Glasgow	G42 8PU	257.29	68.51	583.10
10	Homecare Electrics	6 Arndale Square	Newcastle Upon Tyne	NE12 8SE	504.14	76.19	1172.15
11	Do It Yourself Supplies	84 Church Road	Bristol	BS5 9JY	1550.82	69.12	2742.95
12	Mercury Stores Hdwre Shop	43 Chalcot Road	London	NW1 8LS	607.00	29.89	1094.80
13	Newmans	31 Cherry Tree Avenue	Dover	CT16 2NL	889.70	54.11	1701.70
14	Bob Leach D I Y & Timber Store	101 Botley Road	Southampton	SO52 9DT	1023.00	245.22	2570.40
15	S D I Y Bill Centre	8 Undercliff Road West	Felixstowe	IP11 8AW	929.78	18.39	1915.90
16	D I Y Supplies	17 St James Street	Okehampton	EX20 1DJ	1315.23	233.23	2540.65
17	Pretty Chic	Greenhole Place	Aberdeen	AB23 8EU	300.68	5.18	523.60
18	Manor Utilities Hire Contractors	41 Bridge Road	Southampton	SO2 7DT	357.66	19.79	749.70
19	Fads The Decorating Specialists	Glasgow (Easterhouse)	Glasgow	G34 9DT	261.37	8.39	630.70
20	Murray Timber Supplies Timber & D I Y	3 The Mans	London	NW6 1NY	44.83	0.36	107.10
21	Scotts Hardware D I Y Shop	4 Ellenbrook Green	Ipswich	IP2 9RR	233.41	29.45	446.25
22	Exmouth Handyman	15 Exeter Road	Exmouth	EX8 1PN	820.69	54.67	1469.65
23	G Fox & Sons	139 Clouds Hill Road	Bristol	BS5 7LH	1155.42	248.10	2606.10
24	Do-it-yourself Supplies	35/37 New Street	Carnforth	LA5 9BX	330.56	4.20	672.35
25	Great Mills D I Y Superstore	Rannoch Road	Glasgow	G71 5PR	950.56	204.35	2522.80
26	Sullivans Home Improvement Centre	334 Gloucester Road	Bristol	BS7 8TJ	23.06	3.25	59.50
27	Fads	124 Rye Lane	London	SE15 4RZ	254.75	17.17	464.10
28	Homebase Ltd	Fox Den Road	Bristol	BS12 6SS	984.67	2.16	2403.80
29	Rkp Hardware	51 Englands Lane	London	NW3 4YD	1095.85	5.17	2150.00
30	Walparite	26 Bell Street	Romsey	SO51 8GW	1499.23	59.17	2689.40
31	R Hammersley	44 High Street	Mold	CH7 1BH	76.42	27.80	214.20
32	A G Stanley Ltd	224 Walworth Road	London	SE17 1JE	1011.40	48.16	2112.25
33	Wasons Paint Paper & D I Y Centre	Office	Penarth	CF6 1JD	405.41	26.56	737.80
34	Do It All Limited	Wrexham	Wrexham	LL13 8DH	730.76	19.95	1511.30
35	Sullivans Home Improvement Centre	10 Arnside Road	Bristol	BS10 6AT	732.27	45.24	1570.80
36	D I Y Whitchurch	20 Bell Street	Whitchurch	RG28 7AE	902.22	147.15	1951.60
37	Golders Green D I Y	5 Russell Parade	London	NW11 9NN	165.36	36.98	440.30
38	Timber & Tools	776 Stockport Road	Manchester	M12 4GD	661.73	18.59	1291.15
39	Spectrum Home & Garden Centre	Mold Road	Wrexham	LL12 9UR	894.74	24.88	1594.60
40	Treasure Finder li	Westhill Shopping Centre	Skene	AB32 6RL	894.28	0.00	1987.30
41	Ace Decore Colour & Design Centre	Unit 8 Clarence Street	Chorley	PR7 2AT	1025.06	206.85	2070.60

On the advice of the company's auditors it has now been decided to invest in a proper, integrated accounting system and to transfer the existing records onto this system as soon as possible.

Your Role

It is November 2000, and it is your first week in the office. You have decided that tackling the sales ledger records is your first priority. Besides tidying up the ledgers and eliminating errors and inconsistencies as far as possible you wish to identify and analyse trends that may be helpful to management, for instance to focus their marketing efforts in the right areas, and to improve cash flow.

Note

Marvels Ltd is a fictional company. Although the names of many of the customers in its customer database are names of real DIY suppliers, all of the transactions described are entirely fictitious.

TASKS TO BE COMPLETED

1. Load the spreadsheet filename **DA5_Q,** save it with a name of your own choosing, and improve its general appearance and readability by adding titles, sheet names and formatting as you see fit. **Do not make any changes to the data at this stage**.

2. Devise a coding system and allocate a code number to each customer.

   The names of some customers have been entered inconsistently. For instance Texas are called "Texas Homecare", "Texas Homecare Home Improvements", "Texas Homecare Ltd", and so on.

   Identify and edit out such inconsistencies in your copy of the spreadsheet. If you are not sure that two customers should have the same name, leave both names as they are but make a note of them for further enquiry.

   There are also **four** clear duplicate entries that you must find and **four** possible duplicates. Write a memo to Sami Johnswell, the customer services supervisor, giving him details of the sixteen accounts concerned, so that he can investigate whether the customers concerned are happy for the debts due to be amalgamated.

3. Mr Davis has asked you for some information about geographical sales patterns. Analyse the appropriate data in the spreadsheet and prepare a brief report for Mr Davis providing him with whatever information you think might be useful.

   Make a note of any further discrepancies you find during this exercise, such as missing information, or unusual or erroneous entries.

4. Mr Davis is also concerned about the company's overdraft and would like some information about debtors and cash collection.

   Before you begin make a new copy of your spreadsheet and correct the discrepancies you found in Task 3.

   Then verify that the Total column correctly sums the aged balances. Make a note of any discrepancies. When you have done this assume that the addition has been done incorrectly and recreate the total column using a formula.

You can then analyse the information and summarise your findings in a report to Mr Davis, together with any comments that you feel should be made.

5. Mr Davis has asked Ranju, one of his sales staff, to chase up significant outstanding amounts.

    On a separate sheet prepare a list of debtors with amounts of over £1,500 outstanding for more than 30 days. Include any information that may be useful for Ranju, and any extra columns that may help her in her administration of this task.

6. Although Mr Davis is prepared to follow his auditors' advice he is not sure what an 'integrated accounting system' is. He has asked you to prepare a report on this. In particular you should explain:

    (a) Why the company needs an integrated system.

    (b) What issues need to be considered when transferring data from existing records onto the new system.

BPP PUBLISHING

Trial run devolved assessment
6 Harry Alexander Ltd

Performance criteria

The following performance criteria are covered in this Devolved Assessment.

Element 21.1

Obtain information from a computerised Management Information System

1   The required information is correctly located within the MIS structure

2   Advice is sought where there are difficulties in obtaining the required information

3   Additional authorisation is obtained for sensitive or confidential information in accordance with the organisation's security regulations

4   Information is checked for its accuracy and completeness

5   Information is stored in a format which helps others to access it and use it

6   Confidential information is kept secure and not disclosed to unauthorised people

Element 21.2

Produce spreadsheets for the analysis of numerical information

1   The spreadsheet is titled in a way which clearly defines its use and purpose

2   The arrangement of the spreadsheet is consistent with organisational conventions

3   All rates and other numeric inputs and assumptions are stated to the correct number of decimal places

4   Calculated values are checked for correctness when changes are made to the inputs

5   The spreadsheet is used to carry out data modifications and for entry of related formulas

6   Each cell is formatted clearly and accurately

7   A method is selected to eliminate rounding errors which is suitable for the purpose of the spreadsheet

8   Confidential information is kept secure and not disclosed to unauthorised people

Element 21.3

Contribute to the quality of the Management Information System

1   Potential improvements to the MIS are identified and considered for their impact on the quality of the system and any interrelated systems

2   Suggestions for changes are supported by a clear rationale as to how they could improve the quality of the system

3   The reliability of assumptions and judgements made is assessed and clearly stated

4   The benefits and costs of all changes are described accurately

5   Suggestions are presented clearly and in a way which helps people to understand and act on them

Notes on completing the Simulation

This simulation is designed to test your ability to use a Management Information System.

The situation and tasks are set out for you on pages **59** to **62**.

You are allowed **4 hours** to complete your work.

A high level of accuracy is required. Check your work carefully.

Any spreadsheet that you create should be in good form with proper formatting and making use of a full range of facilities offered. You will not be penalised if the hardware and software tht you use are not the very latest versions. It will not count against you if, for example, you do not have a colour printer or your package does not contain multiple pages.

Attention should be paid to the presentation of your output and reports. You should make full use of the printing facilties, for exmple to make sure that you include proper titles and include headers and footers where appropriate.

Any computer files that are presented for assessment should be on a floppy disk that is clearly marked with your name, the fact that the disk is part of an AAT simulation and the name of the responsible tutor. You should also list the names of the the files on the disk. Filenames should give some indication of their content.

You may either present your answers to the written tasks in handwritten form or as a word processed document if you wish. If you hand write, correcting fluid may be used but it should be used in moderation. Errors should be crossed out neatly and clearly. You should write in black ink, not pencil.

You are advised to read the whole simulation before commencing as all information may be of value and is not necessarly supplied in the sequence in which you would wish to deal with it.

A full solution to this Assessment is provided on page 127. Do not turn to the suggested solution until you have completed all parts of the Assessment.

TRIAL RUN DEVOLVED ASSESSMENT: HARRY ALEXANDER LTD

The situation

Harry Alexander Ltd is a company that carries out restoration work on vintage motor vehicles. The company has between seven and fifteen vehicles being restored on its premises per month.

The company usually charges a single price of £10,000 for a restoration, irrespective of the actual costs incurred, although if a job is clearly going to be particularly difficult the customer is asked to agree to reimburse the company for its costs plus a mark-up on cost of a third.

The work involves quite a considerable amount of labour by skilled mechanics and their assistants and trainees, and also the replacement of a large number of components.

The company has a number of stand-alone Pentium PCs which are used for administrative purposes in the sales, marketing and personnel departments, and to maintain financial accounting records. Costing is done using spreadsheets.

The accounting records

Materials issued from stores are given consecutive issue note numbers of five digits. The issue note records the Job number, the materials code and the quantity issued. Issue notes are pre-numbered and pre-printed with the relevant headings. They are completed manually by stores staff.

Employees are required to record the hours they spend on each job on a job card, which they fill in by hand, usually at the end of each day.

Jobs are then costed for materials and labour by entering data from the issue notes and job cards onto a spreadsheet and applying the relevant costs to each item.

Just before she left the company, your predecessor entered all the issue note information and employee hours for October 2000 into a spreadsheet. Here is an extract to show you how the spreadsheet looks at present.

	A	B	C	D	E	F	G	H	I
1	Issue note	Job	Materials code	Quantity	Materials Cost	Employee	Job	Labour hours	Labour cost
2	47023	728	AH8317	35		P002	726	77	
3	47024	732	TP7325	29		P002	728	67	
4	47025	733	ED2677	51		P002	732	40	
5	47026	731	QE2207	62		P003	726	24	
6	47027	731	YR8218	61		P003	728	40	
7	47028	724	ED2677	57		P003	731	37	
8	47029	724	PF6023	50		P003	733	83	
9	47030	726	XC5229	13		P004	724	42	
10	47031	732	WL5592	13		P004	727	77	
11	47032	729	RK3583	54		P004	731	31	
12	47033	729	ZB2520	1		P004	732	34	
13	47034	728	QE2207	45		P005	724	68	
14	47035	730	YR8218	15		P005	727	61	
15	47036	726	GY2898	6		P005	728	55	
16	47037	729	UQ7049	21		P006	724	34	
17	47038	729	CZ8997	30		P006	726	29	
18	47039	729	DN9569	32		P006	731	79	
19	47040	729	PF6023	53		P006	732	42	

Materials have codes consisting of two letters followed by 4 numbers. For the month of October 2000 the following costs apply.

Material	£
KM6315	8.45
ED2677	8.03
NG7732	6.93
DN9569	6.59
BX3662	5.94
QE2207	5.67
CZ8997	5.38
JV7549	4.35
HU2871	4.00
RK3583	3.60
YR8218	3.44
WL5592	3.29
PF6023	2.81
TP7325	2.34
ZB2520	2.04
VA1662	1.84
UQ7049	1.68
MT9908	1.14
AH8317	1.01
FW4100	0.70
LJ1234	0.66
XC5229	0.59
GY2898	0.27

Employees are given an employee number in the form P001, P002 and so on. Employees are paid at the following hourly rates.

Employee	£
P001	15.00
P002	12.00
P003	12.00
P004	12.00
P005	12.00
P006	12.00
P007	12.00
P008	9.60
P009	9.60
P010	9.60
P011	9.60
P012	7.70
P013	7.70
P014	7.70
P015	7.70
P016	7.70
P017	7.70
P018	7.70
P019	7.70
P020	7.70
P021	7.70
P022	4.80
P023	4.80
P024	3.60

Your Role

You have just been appointed as a cost accountant at Harry Alexander Ltd. The Production Manager has asked you to complete the cost analysis spreadsheet and to provide a variety of information which will be used for determining profitability and to maintain control over the organisation.

The tasks are set out in the next section and you should carry these out in such a way that you can hand over to the Production Manager a package of material (modified spreadsheets, notes, reports and so on) that he can work on over the next few days.

TASKS TO BE COMPLETED

1. Open the spreadsheet **DA6_Q** which is provided as part of the data on the BPP Unit 20 disk. Save the spreadsheet with a name of your own choosing.

   On a separate part of the sheet, or on another sheet, enter the data for materials costs and employee costs (as shown above), and check that you have done so correctly.

2. Making appropriate use of formulae, complete the columns for Materials Cost and Labour Cost. Using the spreadsheet, work out the total materials cost, the total labour cost, and the total cost of materials and labour together.

3. Prepare a report for the Production Manager which includes information on the cost of each job. Make comments, and include a chart or charts, as you feel appropriate, for instance identifying highest and lowest cost, average cost, and so on.

   When you have written your report make notes and queries for your own use about what other information you would like to have so that you can produce more meaningful analyses in the future. These might include comments about the data and/or comments about the nature of the business and the way it is run in general.

4. The Production Manager has asked for some information on the use of materials. In particular he has asked you to have a look at Job 730, which was an almost identical job to Job 718, completed in September 2000, and at material TP7325, of which 520 units were used in September and which he says he would expect to be used in practically equal quantities on every job.

   Here are the details of materials usage for Job 718.

Material	Quantity
AH8317	7
BX3662	36
CZ8997	40
DN9569	22
ED2677	80
FW4100	42
HU2871	5
JV7549	62
KM6315	70
LJ1234	75
MT9908	40
NG7732	60
PF6023	124
QE2207	10
RK3583	50
UQ7049	80
WL5592	34
YR8218	47
ZB2520	149

Prepare a report which provides some useful information on the matter of Job 730 and on the use of material TP7325.

5. The Production Manager also likes to know about the time taken on each job. Prepare a brief note showing which jobs took the longest and shortest times, the average time for each job, and which employee took the longest amount of time on which job.

6. Time was saved because you did not have to enter data regarding issue notes and employee hours into the initial spreadsheet.

The Production Manager has asked you to write a report explaining how the system could be more automated.

The company has been considering investing in a network of PCs for some time. Bear in mind the benefits this might bring (both for cost accounting and for the company as a whole) when you are writing your report, and explain the benefits, and any drawbacks, to the Production Manager.

Trial run devolved assessment
7 Handley Insurance

Performance criteria

The following performance criteria are covered in this Devolved Assessment.

Element 21.1

Obtain information from a computerised Management Information System

1   The required information is correctly located within the MIS structure

2   Advice is sought where there are difficulties in obtaining the required information

3   Additional authorisation is obtained for sensitive or confidential information in accordance with the organisation's security regulations

4   Information is checked for its accuracy and completeness

5   Information is stored in a format which helps others to access it and use it

6   Confidential information is kept secure and not disclosed to unauthorised people

Element 21.2

Produce spreadsheets for the analysis of numerical information

1   The spreadsheet is titled in a way which clearly defines its use and purpose

2   The arrangement of the spreadsheet is consistent with organisational conventions

3   All rates and other numeric inputs and assumptions are stated to the correct number of decimal places

4   Calculated values are checked for correctness when changes are made to the inputs

5   The spreadsheet is used to carry out data modifications and for entry of related formulas

6   Each cell is formatted clearly and accurately

7   A method is selected to eliminate rounding errors which is suitable for the purpose of the spreadsheet

8   Confidential information is kept secure and not disclosed to unauthorised people

Element 21.3

Contribute to the quality of the Management Information System

1   Potential improvements to the MIS are identified and considered for their impact on the quality of the system and any interrelated systems

2   Suggestions for changes are supported by a clear rationale as to how they could improve the quality of the system

3   The reliability of assumptions and judgements made is assessed and clearly stated

4   The benefits and costs of all changes are described accurately

5   Suggestions are presented clearly and in a way which helps people to understand and act on them

BPP
PUBLISHING

Notes on completing the Simulation

This simulation is designed to test your ability to use a Management Information System.

The situation and tasks are set out for you on pages **65** to **68**.

You are allowed **4 hours** to complete your work.

A high level of accuracy is required. Check your work carefully.

Any spreadsheet that you create should be in good form with proper formatting and making use of a full range of facilities offered. You will not be penalised if the hardware and software tht you use are not the very latest versions. It will not count against you if, for example, you do not have a colour printer or your package does not contain multiple pages.

Attention should be paid to the presentation of your output and reports. You should make full use of the printing facilties, for exmple to make sure that you include proper titles and include headers and footers where appropriate.

Any computer files that are presented for assessment should be on a floppy disk that is clearly marked with your name, the fact that the disk is part of an AAT simulation and the name of the responsible tutor. You should also list the names of the the files on the disk. Filenames should give some indication of their content.

You may either present your answers to the written tasks in handwritten form or as a word processed document if you wish. If you hand write, correcting fluid may be used but it should be used in moderation. Errors should be crossed out neatly and clearly. You should write in black ink, not pencil.

You are advised to read the whole simulation before commencing as all information may be of value and is not necessarily supplied in the sequence in which you would wish to deal with it.

A full solution to this Assessment is provided on page 137. Do not turn to the suggested solution until you have completed all parts of the Assessment.

TRIAL RUN DEVOLVED ASSESSMENT 7: HANDLEY INSURANCE

The situation

Handley Insurance is a company specialising in the provision of domestic insurance cover (house contents etc), mainly doing business over the telephone. The business started up in 1994 and has grown steadily since then.

Until 1997 the company occupied a leased office building. In 1997 it purchased Handley House, from which all of its business is now conducted.

The accounting records

Most of the accounting records are kept using a package specially written for insurance companies. However, this package does not feature a fixed assets module and so fixed assets records are kept separately on a spreadsheet, by the Company Secretary's department, which is run by Sarah Handley, wife of the company's founder.

Extract from accounting policies

Depreciation

Tangible assets are depreciated on the following bases.

Buildings	Straight line	50 years
Motor vehicles	Reducing balance	4 years
Furniture and fittings	Straight line	Ten years
Office equipment (except computer equipment)	Straight line	4 years
Computer equipment	Straight line	3 years

A full month's depreciation is provided in the month of purchase (ie an asset bought on, say, 15 July is depreciated at 6/12 times the standard rate in the first year), and none is provided in the month of disposal.

Capitalisation

All purchases of less than £50 are written off during the year of purchase.

The fixed assets spreadsheet was first devised in 1994. It is laid out with the following column headings.

Column	Comment
Date purchased	
Code	Acquisitions are entered in order of purchase date and are coded sequentially, numbering upwards from 1.
Description 1	
Description 2	
Description 3	
Serial number	
Location/Employee	
Supplier	
Asset Category	FF = Furniture and fittings, OM = Office machinery, V = Vehicles, LB = Land and buildings
Department	
Depn method	S = Straight line, R = Reducing balance
Depn rate	
Cost price	
Depn to date	
Book value	

Your Role

It is early 2001 and you have been employed on a temporary basis to get the accounting records ready for audit.

You have been asked to examine the fixed assets records, update them for the year ended 31 December 2000, and suggest or make improvements to the system wherever possible.

TASKS TO BE COMPLETED

1. Load the spreadsheet filename **DA7_Q**, save it with a name of your own choosing, and improve its general appearance and readability by adding titles, sheet names and formatting as you see fit. **Do not make any changes to the data at this stage**.

2. The file you have been given includes invoices for the items listed below which Peter Worthington, a junior and inexperienced member of the accounts department, has identified as fixed assets but which have not yet been entered into the spreadsheet.

Date purchased	20/10/2000
Item	Lexus Laser 353
Serial number	
Supplier	Simply Computers
Cost price	£649

Date purchased	24/10/2000
Item	Desk lamp, Red, Argley 60 watts,
Serial number	P42-4752
Supplier	Argos
Cost price	£22.99

Date purchased	01/11/2000
Item	Ford Escort 1.6, Blue metallic
Serial number	R452 PJX
Supplier	Harwoods
Cost price	£8,995

Date purchased	14/11/2000
Item	Microsoft Office 97 (10 copies)
Serial number	Various
Supplier	Jens Supplies
Cost price	£2,980

Date purchased	17/11/2000
Item	Lift (gas)
Serial number	JX-4713
Supplier	ErgoFurn
Cost price	£143.99

Date purchased	5/12/2000
Item	Computer 400MHz
Serial number	CQ4-521389
Supplier	Compaq
Cost price	£1,854.99

Date purchased	5/12/2000
Item	Screen/partition
Serial number	
Supplier	
Cost price	£185.00

Date purchased	24/12/2000
Item	Sanyo Playstation
Serial number	
Supplier	Argos
Cost price	£299.99

Update the spreadsheet as appropriate. You will need to allocate code numbers and decide on asset category, depreciation method and rate and so on, based on what you have read above and can see in the spreadsheet.

Do not make up information if it is missing . If you have any queries make a note of them, and then write a memo to the junior accountant, explaining what your queries are and asking for any additional information you think you need, and making any other points that you think he needs to know about.

3. Look through the records in the spreadsheet and identify any items that you think are unusual or wrong. To help you with this you may find it useful to sort or filter the data according to various criteria, for instance looking for negative balances, or unusual supplier names, or unexpected locations. Duplicates could be found by sorting the data according to serial number.

    Write a memo to Sarah Handley outlining any concerns you may have.

    Assume that your concerns are correct and remove any items that should not be in the fixed assets spreadsheet, making a note of your reasons. Do not re-code the assets that remain.

4. According to a letter from the auditors dated 14 October 2000, the amount shown for depreciation to date on nearly all of the motor vehicles has been wrongly calculated.

    Extract the data as necessary from your spreadsheet created for Task 3, and devise a separate spreadsheet that recalculates the depreciation correctly. Also, calculate the amount that should be provided for 2000.

    Prepare a letter to the auditors giving them full details of the discrepancies that you have found in the cumulative depreciation figures for motor vehicles. The auditor's name and address are as follows.

Meat Parwick
24, Apple Road.
London,
N12 3PP

5. Enter your revised figures for vehicle depreciation into your version of the main spreadsheet (from Task 3).

Now check that depreciation on all other assets has been correctly provided, doing your calculation on the following basis.

(Days between 31/12/99 and purchase date)/365 * Cost price * Depreciation rate

Ignore differences that are less than 10% of the amount of depreciation currently provided, but make a note of any assets whose depreciation has been calculated wrongly. Correct your main spreadsheet accordingly.

Finally, in a new column, provide depreciation for the year ended 31 December 2000 on all assets (you have already done this for vehicles in task 4), and calculate the cumulative depreciation for each asset and their net book values for the year ended 31 December 2000.

6. Prepare the fixed assets note for the accounts for the year ended 31 December 2000. The fixed assets note should be prepared in the following form. Note that there were no disposals in the year. You should of course fill in figures where indicated by Xs.

	Total £	Land and buildings £	Motor vehicles £	Furniture and fittings £	Office machinery £
Cost or valuation					
At 1 January 2000	X	X	X	X	X
Additions in year	X	X	X	X	X
At 31 December 2000	X	X	X	X	X
Depreciation					
At 1 January 2000	X	X	X	X	X
Charge for year	X	X	X	X	X
At 31 December 2000	X	X	X	X	X
Net book value					
At 31 December 2000	X	X	X	X	X
At 1 January 2000	X	X	X	X	X

7. No records are presently kept on the **use** of assets, for instance vehicle mileage, petrol expenditure or repairs to vehicles or office equipment. You have suggested to Sarah Handley that it might be useful to devise an 'executive information system' for this purpose.

Sarah likes the sound of this, but she does not know what an executive information system is.

Prepare a memo to Sarah that explains the various kinds of information system in use in a typical organisation, and suggest what items of information the Fixed Assets EIS could contain and how it might be used.

Solutions to Practice Activities

SOLUTIONS TO PRACTICE ACTIVITIES

Note. Suggested solutions to the practice activities are set out below. There are often different ways to reach a satisfactory solution to an activity and there may be no single right answer. Having completed the activities for yourself, compare your approach to ours and identify any errors you may have made.

Solution to Activity 1

The spreadsheet uses the LOOKUP function to match up the data in cell D3 with the corresponding data in cells C11 to C14. Cell D4 displays the value in the cell to the right of the cell in C11:C14 that matches the data in cell D3.

In other words if you tell the spreadsheet a person's name it looks up their age.

The formula used to do this is **=LOOKUP(D3,C11:D14)**

Solution to Activity 2

The solution will be found in the file **Ac_02_S** which is protected by a password: **lookout**

Make sure you do not have your Caps Lock key on when you type the password. In this case you should type lower case letters only.

The total charge is £7,899.00.

The formula to use in column H is **=LOOKUP(F2,$A$2:$B$6)*G2**. You can then fill down the remaining rows and sum the column using the SUM function.

Solution to Activity 3

The solution is shown on the next page.

The file is available as **Ac_03_S** in the directory where you are storing your BPP data files. The password is **ETB**

Make sure you type capitals when entering the password this time.

Account		Trial balance £	£	Adjustments £	£	Accrued £	Prepaid £	Profit and loss £	£	Balance sheet £	£
Sales	P		(336,247)					0	(336,247)	0	0
Purchases	P	224,362		1,624				225,986	0	0	0
Carriage	P	6,184			(1,624)			4,560	0	0	0
Drawings	B	14,686						0	0	14,686	0
Rent and rates	P	14,621				510	(2,120)	13,011	0	0	0
Postage and stationery	P	5,789						5,789	0	0	0
Advertising	P	2,941						2,941	0	0	0
Salaries and wages	P	56,934						56,934	0	0	0
Bad debt expense	P	1,614		256				1,870	0	0	0
Provision for Bad Debts	B		(365)		(256)			0	0	0	(621)
Debtors	B	31,050						0	0	31,050	0
Creditors	B		(9,456)					0	0	0	(9,456)
Cash in hand	B	422						0	0	422	0
Cash at bank	B	2,136						0	0	2,136	0
Stock as at 1 July 20X5	P	15,605						15,605	0	0	0
Equipment	B	116,000						0	0	116,000	0
Depreciation	B		(55,400)		(17,400)			0	0	0	(72,800)
Capital	B		(90,876)					0	0	0	(90,876)
Prepaymets	B					2,120		0	0	2,120	0
Accruals	B						(510)	0	0	0	(510)
Depreciation expense	P			17,400				17,400	0	0	0
Closing stock	B			31,529				0	0	31,529	
Closing stock	P				(31,529)			0	(31,529)	0	0
								0	0	0	0
SUB-TOTAL		492,344	(492,344)	50,809	(50,809)	2,630	(2,630)	344,096	(367,776)	197,943	(174,263)
Profit for the year								23,680	0	0	(23,680)
TOTAL		492,344	(492,344)	50,809	(50,809)	2,630	(2,630)	367,776	(367,776)	197,943	(197,943)

Dunraven
ETB Year Ended 30/06/20X6

Solution to Activity 4

The solution is shown below.

Dunraven
ETB Year Ended 30/06/20X6

Account		Trial balance £	£	Adjustments £	£	Accrued £	Prepaid £	Profit and loss £	£	Balance sheet £	£
Sales	P		(336,247)					0	(336,247)	0	0
Purchases	P	224,362		1,624				225,986	0	0	0
Carriage	P	6,184			(1,624)			4,560	0	0	0
Drawings	B	14,686						0	0	14,686	0
Rent and rates	P	14,621				510	(2,120)	13,011	0	0	0
Postage and stationery	P	5,789						5,789	0	0	0
Advertising	P	2,941						2,941	0	0	0
Salaries and wages	P	56,934						56,934	0	0	0
Bad debt expense	P	1,614		256				1,870	0	0	0
Provision for Bad Debts	B		(365)		(256)			0	0	0	(621)
Debtors	B	31,050						0	0	31,050	0
Creditors	B		(9,456)					0	0	0	(9,456)
Cash in hand	B	422						0	0	422	0
Cash at bank	B	2,136						0	0	2,136	0
Stock as at 1 July 20X5	P	15,605						15,605	0	0	0
Equipment	B	116,000						0	0	116,000	0
Depreciation	B		(55,400)		(23,200)			0	0	0	(78,600)
Capital	B		(90,876)					0	0	0	(90,876)
Prepaymets	B					2,120		0	0	2,120	0
Accruals	B						(510)	0	0	0	(510)
Depreciation expense	P			23,200				23,200	0	0	0
Closing stock	B			31,529				0	0	31,529	
Closing stock	P				(31,529)			0	(31,529)	0	0
								0	0	0	0
SUB-TOTAL		492,344	(492,344)	56,609	(56,609)	2,630	(2,630)	349,896	(367,776)	197,943	(180,063)
Profit for the year								17,880	0	0	(17,880)
TOTAL		492,344	(492,344)	56,609	(56,609)	2,630	(2,630)	367,776	(367,776)	197,943	(197,943)

Solution to Activity 5

The solution is shown below. This is **not** provided on disk, since we are trying to encourage you to develop a spreadsheet from scratch, or else using one of your own old models.

	A	B	C	D	E	F	G	H	I	J	K	L
1	Oaklands											
2	ETB Year Ended 30/12/20X4											
3	Account		Trial balance		Adjustments		Accrued	Prepaid	Profit and loss		Balance sheet	
4			£	£	£	£	£	£	£	£	£	£
5												
6	Capital	B		(44,550)								(44,550)
7	Freehold L & B	B	25,000								25,000	
8	F & F: cost	B	3,360								3,360	
9	F & F: depn	B		(2,016)		(336)						(2,352)
10	MV: cost	B	1,900								1,900	
11	MV: depn	B		(980)		(380)						(1,210)
12	Purchases	P	101,286						101,286			
13	Sales	P		(142,125)						(142,125)		
14	Rent received	P		(810)		(268)				(1,078)		
15	Drawings	B	9,732								9,732	
16	Car expenses	P	841						841			
17	Stock at 1.1.20X4	P	10,858						10,858			
18	Bad debt expense	P	943			(147)			796			
19	Prov' doubtful debts at 1.1.20X4	B		(792)	147							(645)
20	General expenses	P	1,842					(86)	1,756			
21	Rent and rates	P	2,414					(106)	2,308			
22	Trade debtors	B	16,121								16,121	
23	Trade creditors	B		(9,125)								(9,125)
24	Wages and salaries	P	18,103				421		18,524			
25	Discounts allowed	P	3,125						3,125			
26	Bank	B	4,873								4,873	
27	Stock at 31.12.20X4	B			12,654					(12,654)	12,654	
28	Stock at 31.12.20X4	P				(12,654)						
29	Accruals	B					(421)					(421)
30	Prepayments	B						192			192	
31	Depreciation expense	P			716				716			
32	Sundry debtors	B			268						268	
33												
34												
35	SUB-TOTAL		200,398	(200,398)	13,785	(13,785)	613	(613)	140,210	(155,857)	74,100	(58,303)
36	Profit for the year								15,647	0	0	(15,647)
37	TOTAL		200,398	(200,398)	13,785	(13,785)	613	(613)	155,857	(155,857)	74,100	(73,950)

Solution to Activity 6

The solution to Activity 6 is shown below.

You need to amend the formula for the depreciation provision as follows.

=(C10+D11)*0.25

	A	B	C	D	E	F	G	H	I	J	K	L
1	Oaklands											
2	ETB Year Ended 30/12/20X4											
3	Account		Trial balance		Adjustments		Accrued	Prepaid	Profit and loss		Balance sheet	
4			£	£	£	£	£	£	£	£	£	£
5												
6	Capital	B		(44,550)								(44,550)
7	Freehold L & B	B	25,000								25,000	
8	F & F: cost	B	3,360								3,360	
9	F & F: depn	B		(2,016)		(336)						(2,352)
10	MV: cost	B	1,900								1,900	
11	MV: depn	B		(980)		(230)						(1,210)
12	Purchases	P	101,286						101,286			
13	Sales	P		(142,125)						(142,125)		
14	Rent received	P		(810)		(268)				(1,078)		
15	Drawings	B	9,732								9,732	
16	Car expenses	P	841						841			
17	Stock at 1.1.20X4	P	10,858						10,858			
18	Bad debt expense	P	943			(147)			796			
19	Prov' doubtful debts at 1.1.20X4	B		(792)	147							(645)
20	General expenses	P	1,842					(86)	1,756			
21	Rent and rates	P	2,414					(106)	2,308			
22	Trade debtors	B	16,121								16,121	
23	Trade creditors	B		(9,125)								(9,125)
24	Wages and salaries	P	18,103				421		18,524			
25	Discounts allowed	P	3,125						3,125			
26	Bank	B	4,873								4,873	
27	Stock at 31.12.20X4	B			12,654					(12,654)	12,654	
28	Stock at 31.12.20X4	P				(12,654)						
29	Accruals	B					(421)					(421)
30	Prepayments	B						192			192	
31	Depreciation expense	P			566				566			
32	Sundry debtors	B			268						268	
33												
34												
35	SUB-TOTAL		200,398	(200,398)	13,635	(13,635)	613	(613)	140,060	(155,857)	74,100	(58,303)
36	Profit for the year								15,797	0	0	(15,797)
37	TOTAL		200,398	(200,398)	13,635	(13,635)	613	(613)	155,857	(155,857)	74,100	(74,100)

Solution to Activity 7

Here are the formulae in Excel.

	A	B	C	D
1	36945	=DAY(A1)	=MONTH(A1)	=YEAR(A1)
2	37256	=DAY(A2)	=MONTH(A2)	=YEAR(A2)
3	=A2-A1			

The dates in column A have been formatted (using the custom option) as dd/mm/yyyy. Subtracting dates from one another shows the number of days between the two dates, in this case 311.

Solution to Activity 8

A full solution is shown on the next page.

The formulae used in this spreadsheet are as follows.

	A	B	C	D	E	F
1	**Goodwood Furniture**					
2	**Overhead apportionment**					
3	*Budget*					
4						
28						
29	**Apportionment calculation**					
30	*Overhead*					
31		*Dept A*	*Dept B*	*Dept C*	*Dept X*	*Dept Y*
32	Costs specific to each dept	=B25	=C25	=D25	=E25	=F25
33	Rent and rates	=B8*B18/SUM(B18:F18)	=B8*C18/SUM(B18:F18)	=B8*D18/SUM(B18:F18)	=B8*E18/SUM(B18:F18)	=B8*F18/SUM(B18:F18)
34	Machine insurance	=B9*B19/SUM(B19:F19)	=B9*C19/SUM(B19:F19)	=B9*D19/SUM(B19:F19)	=B9*E19/SUM(B19:F19)	=B9*F19/SUM(B19:F19)
35	Telephone charges	=B10*B18/SUM(B18:F18)	=B10*C18/SUM(B18:F18)	=B10*D18/SUM(B18:F18)	=B10*E18/SUM(B18:F18)	=B10*F18/SUM(B18:F18)
36	Depreciation	=B11*B19/SUM(B19:F19)	=B11*C19/SUM(B19:F19)	=B11*D19/SUM(B19:F19)	=B11*E19/SUM(B19:F19)	=B11*F19/SUM(B19:F19)
37	Production supervisor	=B12*B20/SUM(B20:D20)	=B12*C20/SUM(B20:D20)	=B12*D20/SUM(B20:D20)		
38	Heat and light	=B13*B18/SUM(B18:F18)	=B13*C18/SUM(B18:F18)	=B13*D18/SUM(B18:F18)	=B13*E18/SUM(B18:F18)	=B13*F18/SUM(B18:F18)
39		=SUM(B32:B38)	=SUM(C32:C38)	=SUM(D32:D38)	=SUM(E32:E38)	=SUM(F32:F38)
40	Apportionment of costs of Dept X	=E39*B26	=E39*C26	=E39*D26		
41	Apportionment of costs of Dept Y	=F39*B27	=F39*C27	=F39*D27		
42		=SUM(B39:B41)	=SUM(C39:C41)	=SUM(D39:D41)		
43						
44	**Absorption rate**					
45		*Dept A*	*Dept B*	*Dept C*		
46		£	£	£		
47	Rate per labour hour	=B42/B20	=C42/C20	=D42/D20		
48						

	A	B	C	D	E	F
1	**Goodwood Furniture**					
2	**Overhead apportionment**					
3	*Budget*					
4						
5						
6	*Total overheads*					
7		£				
8	Rent and rates	12,800				
9	Machine insurance	6,000				
10	Telephone charges	3,200				
11	Depreciation	18,000				
12	Production supervisor	24,000				
13	Heat and light	6,400				
14		70,400				
15						
16	*Departmental statistics*					
17		*Dept A*	*Dept B*	*Dept C*	*Dept X*	*Dept Y*
18	Floor area (sq. m)	3,000	1,800	600	600	400
19	Machine value (£)	24,000	10,000	8,000	4,000	2,000
20	Direct labour hours	3,200	1,800	1,000		
21	Labour rates/hour (£)	3.80	3.50	3.40	3.00	3.00
22						
23	*Allocated overheads*					
24		*Dept A*	*Dept B*	*Dept C*		
25	Specific to each department	2,800	1,700	1,200	800	600
26	Apportionment of costs of Dept	50%	25%	25%		
27	Apportionment of costs of Dept	20%	30%	50%		
28						
29	**Apportionment calculation**					
30	*Overhead*					
31		*Dept A*	*Dept B*	*Dept C*	*Dept X*	*Dept Y*
32	Costs specific to each dept	2,800	1,700	1,200	800	600
33	Rent and rates	6000	3600	1200	1200	800
34	Machine insurance	3000	1250	1000	500	250
35	Telephone charges	1500	900	300	300	200
36	Depreciation	9000	3750	3000	1500	750
37	Production supervisor	12800	7200	4000		
38	Heat and light	3000	1800	600	600	400
39		38,100	20,200	11,300	4,900	3,000
40	Apportionment of costs of Dept	2450	1225	1225		
41	Apportionment of costs of Dept	600	900	1500		
42		41,150	22,325	14,025		
43						
44	**Absorption rate**					
45		*Dept A*	*Dept B*	*Dept C*		
46		£	£	£		
47	Rate per labour hour	12.86	12.40	14.03		
48						

Solution to Activity 9

The spreadsheet would appear as follows. In this situation you could use cells as a 'calculator', for example, cell B8 could be changed from 12,800 to =12,800*1.05, and so on.

Better (and you should now be firmly in the habit of never mixing up cell references and 'real' numbers in formulae), is to *copy* the values in cells B8 to B13 into cells D8 to D13, enter the changes (1.05, 1.10 etc) in cells C8 to C13, and then change the values in B8 to B13 to formulae:=C8*D8 and so on. This would be the 'Advanced' answer, so well done if you got this.

	A	B	C	D	E	F
1	**Goodwood Furniture**					
2	**Overhead apportionment**					
3	*Budget*					
4						
5		1.05				
6	*Total overheads*					
7		£	*Change*	*Revised*		
8	Rent and rates	13,440	1.05	12,800		
9	Machine insurance	6,600	1.10	6,000		
10	Telephone charges	4,000	1.25	3,200		
11	Depreciation	18,000	1	18,000		
12	Production supervisor	24,672	1.028	24,000		
13	Heat and light	5,888	0.92	6,400		
14		72,600		70,400		
15						
16	*Departmental statistics*					
17		*Dept A*	*Dept B*	*Dept C*	*Dept X*	*Dept Y*
18	Floor area (sq. m)	3,000	1,800	600	600	400
19	Machine value (£)	24,000	10,000	8,000	4,000	2,000
20	Direct labour hours	3,200	1,800	1,000		
21	Labour rates/hour (£)	3.80	3.50	3.40	3.00	3.00
22						
23	*Allocated overheads*					
24		*Dept A*	*Dept B*	*Dept C*		
25	Specific to each department	2,800	1,700	1,200	800	600
26	Apportionment of costs of Dept	50%	25%	25%		
27	Apportionment of costs of Dept	20%	30%	50%		
28						
29	**Apportionment calculation**					
30	*Overhead*					
31		*Dept A*	*Dept B*	*Dept C*	*Dept X*	*Dept Y*
32	Costs specific to each dept	2,800	1,700	1,200	800	600
33	Rent and rates	6300	3780	1260	1260	840
34	Machine insurance	3300	1375	1100	550	275
35	Telephone charges	1875	1125	375	375	250
36	Depreciation	9000	3750	3000	1500	750
37	Production supervisor	13158.4	7401.6	4112		
38	Heat and light	2760	1656	552	552	368
39		39,193	20,788	11,599	5,037	3,083
40	Apportionment of costs of Dept	2518.5	1259.25	1259.25		
41	Apportionment of costs of Dept	616.6	924.9	1541.5		
42		42,329	22,972	14,400		
43						
44	**Absorption rate**					
45		*Dept A*	*Dept B*	*Dept C*		
46		£	£	£		
47	Rate per labour hour	13.23	12.76	14.40		
48						

Solution to Activity 10

(a) There will not usually be time to check *all* the formulae in a spreadsheet but most of them will be simple copies filled down or across. The best way to approach this is to 'spot check' the first formula in a range by performing the calculation manually. The rest should be scanned to see if they give results which appear reasonable and checked fully if not.

(b) (i) Saving and back-up.

(ii) Cell protection.

(c) (i)   Authorisation. Only certain people should be allowed access to the spreadsheet. Disks should be kept locked up and be accessible only on production of an authorised form.

(ii)   Passwords.

(iii)   Hidden format.

Solution to Activity 11

(a)   Any *six* of the following.

- Relevant for its purpose
- Complete for its purpose
- Clear to the user
- Concise
- Produced at the appropriate time
- Provided at a cost which is less than the value of the benefits
- Communicated to the right person
- As accurate as necessary

(b)   In general the benefit obtainable from the information must exceed the cost of obtaining it. Information which saves £50 is not cost-effective if it costs £60 to collect.

For information to have value, it must lead to a decision taken which results in an improvement, such as a reduction in costs or an increase in sales. Even information which persuades management not to take an inappropriate decision is therefore of some value.

The greater the accuracy of the information, the more it will cost. A high level of accuracy may not always be necessary in order to make a decision and may therefore be a waste of time and money. In the case of budgets, for example, accuracy to the nearest penny is unnecessary and is in any case rarely, if ever, possible.

(c)   The practicalities of obtaining information will depend on the circumstances. However, the following principles will always apply.

(i)   Information should be obtained with as little as possible disruption to others. This involves forward planning to ensure that the information is not requested at the last minute from someone who is very busy with other tasks.

(ii)   If the person producing the report requires access to information not normally disclosed to him, authorisation must be obtained at the appropriate level and well in advance.

(d)   Information for use in spreadsheets may be obtained from:

- Within the existing computerised Management Information System (MIS)
- Within the organisation but not the computerised MIS
- Outside the organisation, eg from published reports
- The user's own assumptions and estimates

Solution to Activity 12

We strongly encourage you to learn how to use the Pivot Table facility. It is on of the most widely used spreadsheet functions and you may find it useful in your Devolved Assessment.

To look at, or play with, a spreadsheet that has a Pivot Table in it already, open the file **Ac_12_S** in your **BPPU21** directory. The password is:

useful

To have a look at how this has been set up you can right click with your mouse in a cell in the Pivot Table. A menu like the following menu will appear.

	A	B	C	D	E	F	G
1	Sum of Quantity	Colour					
2	Shape	Blue	Green	Red	Yellow	Grand Total	
3	Round	482	584	297	824	2187	
4	Square	628	1440	1240	1153	4461	
5	Triangular	1195	1139	1114	7		
6	Grand Total	2305	3163	2651	27		
7							
8							
9							
10							
11							
12							
13							
14							
15							
16							
17							
18							
19							
20							

Menu options shown:
- Format Cells...
- Insert
- Delete
- Wizard...
- Refresh Data
- Select ▶
- Group and Outline ▶
- Formulas ▶
- Field...
- Options...
- Show Pages...

Select the **Wizard ...** option and you will be taken back to the layout stage of the Pivot Table production process.

Solution to Activity 13

(a) and (b)

We have set up the balance sheet and profit and loss account as part of the spreadsheet. This means that any changes, for example to the opening balance sheet, can be included with minimal re-input.

(c) to (i) The variables to be entered are as follows.

	A	B	C	D	E
28					
29	**Opening B/Sheet**	£'000			
30	Land and buildings	220			
31	Plant and machinery	110			
32	Motor vehicles	65			
33	Stock	40			
34	Trade debtors	60			
35	Cash in hand	5			
36	Overdraft	-65			
37	Trade creditors	-35			
38	Long term creditors	-120			
39		=SUM(B30:B38)			
40					
41	**P & L Account**	£'000	July	Aug	Sept
42	Sales	390	=$B$42*B53	=$B$42*B53	=$B$42*$B$54
43	Purchases	-165	=$B$43/12		
44	Rent and rates	-60			
45	Depreciation	-30			
46	Marketing	-35			
47	Administrative expenses	-75			
48	Selling expenses	-45			
49	Profit/loss before interest	=SUM(B42:B48)			
50					
51					
52	**Other data required**				
53	Sales July/August	=1/6			
54	Sales other months	=(1-(2*B53))/10			
55	Debtor collection (Mth 0)	0.1			
56	Debtor collection (Mth 1)	0.6			
57	Debtor collection (Mth 2)	0.3			
58	Opening debtors collection	0.9			
59	Creditors payment (Mth 0)	0.2			
60	Creditors payment (Mth 1)	0.8			
61	Rates	-20			
62	Rent per quarter	=(B44-B61)/4			
63	Marketing per month	-1			
64	Marketing burst (Nov)	=B46-(11*B63)			
65	Admin expenses	=B47/12			
66	Monthly interest rate (o'draft)	0.02			
67					

Here are the numbers you should have got.

	A	B	C	D	E	F	G	H	I	J	K	L	M	N
1	**Rolling Projections Ltd**													
2	**Cash flow forecast**													
3	**Year ending 30 June 20X6**	July	Aug	Sept	Oct	Nov	Dec	Jan	Feb	Mar	April	May	June	Total
4		£'000	£'000	£'000	£'000	£'000	£'000	£'000	£'000	£'000	£'000	£'000	£'000	£'000
5	**Cash inflows**													
6	Opening debtors	54.00												54.00
7	Month of sale	6.50	6.50	2.60	2.60	2.60	2.60	2.60	2.60	2.60	2.60	2.60	2.60	39.00
8	1 month		39.00	39.00	15.60	15.60	15.60	15.60	15.60	15.60	15.60	15.60	15.60	218.40
9	2 months			19.50	19.50	7.80	7.80	7.80	7.80	7.80	7.80	7.80	7.80	101.40
10	Total receipts	60.50	45.50	61.10	37.70	26.00	26.00	26.00	26.00	26.00	26.00	26.00	26.00	412.80
11														
12	**Cash outflows**													
13	Opening creditors		-35.00											-35.00
14	Month of purchase	-2.75	-2.75	-2.75	-2.75	-2.75	-2.75	-2.75	-2.75	-2.75	-2.75	-2.75	-2.75	-33.00
15	1 month		-11.00	-11.00	-11.00	-11.00	-11.00	-11.00	-11.00	-11.00	-11.00	-11.00	-11.00	-121.00
16	Rent			-10.00			-10.00			-10.00			-10.00	-40.00
17	Rates										-20.00			-20.00
18	Marketing	-1.00	-1.00	-1.00	-1.00	-24.00	-1.00	-1.00	-1.00	-1.00	-1.00	-1.00	-1.00	-35.00
19	Administrative expenses	-6.25	-6.25	-6.25	-6.25	-6.25	-6.25	-6.25	-6.25	-6.25	-6.25	-6.25	-6.25	-75.00
20	Selling expenses	-7.50	-7.50	-3.00	-3.00	-3.00	-3.00	-3.00	-3.00	-3.00	-3.00	-3.00	-3.00	-45.00
21	Total payments	-17.50	-63.50	-34.00	-24.00	-47.00	-34.00	-24.00	-24.00	-34.00	-44.00	-24.00	-34.00	-404.00
22														
23	Net cash flow	43.00	-18.00	27.10	13.70	-21.00	-8.00	2.00	2.00	-8.00	-18.00	2.00	-8.00	8.80
24	Blance b/f	-65.00	-22.44	-41.25	-14.43	-0.75	-22.18	-30.78	-29.36	-27.91	-36.63	-55.72	-54.79	-65.00
25	Balance c/f (pre Interest)	-22.00	-40.44	-14.15	-0.73	-21.75	-30.18	-28.78	-27.36	-35.91	-54.63	-53.72	-62.79	-56.20
26	Interest	-0.44	-0.81	-0.28	-0.01	-0.43	-0.60	-0.58	-0.55	-0.72	-1.09	-1.07	-1.26	-7.85
27	Balance c/f (post Interest)	-22.44	-41.25	-14.43	-0.75	-22.18	-30.78	-29.36	-27.91	-36.63	-55.72	-54.79	-64.05	-64.05
28														

BPP
PUBLISHING

The formulae that we have used are indicated in the extract below.

	A	B	C	D	E	F
1	Rolling Projections Lt					
2	Cash flow forecast					
3	Year ending 30 June	July	Aug	Sept	Oct	Nov
4		£'000	£'000	£'000	£'000	£'000
5	Cash inflows					
6	Opening debtors	=$B$34*B58				
7	Month of sale	=C42*$B$55	=D42*$B$55	=$E$42*$B$55	=$E$42*$B$55	=$E$42*$B$55
8	1 month		=C42*$B$56	=D42*$B$56	=$E$42*$B$56	=$E$42*$B$56
9	2 months			=C42*$B$57	=D42*$B$57	=$E$42*$B$57
10	Total receipts	=SUM(B6:B9)	=SUM(C6:C9)	=SUM(D6:D9)	=SUM(E6:E9)	=SUM(F6:F9)
11						
12	Cash outflows					
13	Opening creditors		=B37			
14	Month of purchase	=$C$43*$B$59	=$C$43*$B$59	=$C$43*$B$59	=$C$43*$B$59	=$C$43*$B$59
15	1 month		=$C$43*$B$60	=$C$43*$B$60	=$C$43*$B$60	=$C$43*$B$60
16	Rent			=B62		
17	Rates					
18	Marketing	=$B$63	=$B$63	=$B$63	=$B$63	=B64
19	Administrative expenses	=$B$65	=$B$65	=$B$65	=$B$65	=$B$65
20	Selling expenses	=$B$48*$B$53	=$B$48*$B$53	=$B$48*$B$54	=$B$48*$B$54	=$B$48*$B$54
21	Total payments	=SUM(B13:B20)	=SUM(C13:C20)	=SUM(D13:D20)	=SUM(E13:E20)	=SUM(F13:F20)
22						
23	Net cash flow	=B10+B21	=C10+C21	=D10+D21	=E10+E21	=F10+F21
24	Balance b/f	=B36	=B27	=C27	=D27	=E27
25	Balance c/f (pre interest)	=SUM(B23:B24)	=SUM(C23:C24)	=SUM(D23:D24)	=SUM(E23:E24)	=SUM(F23:F24)
26	Interest	=IF(B25<0,B25*$B$66,0)	=IF(C25<0,C25*$B$66,0)	=IF(D25<0,D25*$B$66,0)	=IF(E25<0,E25*$B$66,0)	=IF(F25<0,F25*$B$66,0)
27	Balance c/f (post interest)	=SUM(B25:B26)	=SUM(C25:C26)	=SUM(D25:D26)	=SUM(E25:E26)	=SUM(F25:F26)

Solution to Activity 14

We have tackled this by inserting five rows immediately beneath the relevant section of the spreadsheet. (This does not affect the lower part of the spreadsheet - check the formulae for yourself.)

	A	B	C	D	E	F	G	H	I	J	K	L	M	N
27	Balance c/f (post Interest)	-22.44	-41.25	-14.43	-0.75	-22.18	-30.78	-29.36	-27.91	-36.63	-55.72	-54.79	-64.05	-64.05
28														
29	Overdraft facility													
30	Amount of facility	-50.00												
31	Faciltiy exceeded?	No	No	No	No	No	No	No	No	No	Yes	Yes	Yes	
32	Headroom/(excess)	27.56	8.75	35.57	49.25	27.82	19.22	20.64	22.09	13.37	-5.72	-4.79	-14.05	

The formulae which we have used for this are as follows. They have been copied right across to the June column.

	A	B	C	D	
27	Balance c/f (post Interest)	=SUM(B25:B26)	=SUM(C25:C26)	=SUM(D25:D26)	
28					
29	Overdraft facility				
30	Amount of facility	-50			
31	Faciltiy exceeded?	=IF($B$30>B27, "Yes", "No")	=IF($B$30>C27, "Yes", "No")	=IF($B$30>D27, "Yes", "No")	
32	Headroom/(excess)	=B27-$B$30	=C27-$B$30	=D27-$B$30	

Solution to Activity 15

(a) The 'skeleton' spreadsheet is shown below. We ignored the rather strange order in which the data was presented, ie latest week first and worked from left to right with time, which would make any necessary extension of the spreadsheet slightly easier. (Of course, you could extend it if you had started with week 3: you would need to *insert* new columns to the left of week 3.)

	A	B	C	D	E	F
1	**Special assignment**					
2	Personnel Costs					
3		**Week 1**	**Week 2**	**Week 3**	**Total**	
4		Cost	Cost	Cost	Cost	
5		£	£	£	£	
6	Divisional chief accountant	0.00	0.00	0.00	0.00	
7	Assistant accountant	0.00	0.00	0.00	0.00	
8	Accounting technician	0.00	0.00	0.00	0.00	
9	Secretary	0.00	0.00	0.00	0.00	
10	Total cost	0.00	0.00	0.00	0.00	
11						
12		Hours	Hours	Hours	Hours	
13	Divisional chief accountant				0.00	
14	Assistant accountant				0.00	
15	Accounting technician				0.00	
16	Secretary				0.00	
17	Total	0.00	0.00	0.00	0.00	
18						
19	*Chargeout rates*					
20	Divisional chief accountant	72.50	72.50	72.50		
21	Assistant accountant	38.00	38.00	38.00		
22	Accounting technician	21.45	21.45	21.45		
23	Secretary	17.30	17.30	17.30		
24						

The underlying formulae are as follows.

	A	B	C	D	E
1	**Special assignment**				
2	Personnel Costs				
3		**Week 1**	**Week 2**	**Week 3**	**Total**
4		Cost	Cost	Cost	Cost
5		£	£	£	£
6	Divisional chief accountant	=B13*B20	=C13*C20	=D13*D20	=SUM(B6:D6)
7	Assistant accountant	=B14*B21	=C14*C21	=D14*D21	=SUM(B7:D7)
8	Accounting technician	=B15*B22	=C15*C22	=D15*D22	=SUM(B8:D8)
9	Secretary	=B16*B23	=C16*C23	=D16*D23	=SUM(B9:D9)
10	Total cost	=SUM(B6:B9)	=SUM(C6:C9)	=SUM(D6:D9)	=SUM(E6:E9)
11					
12		Hours	Hours	Hours	Hours
13	Divisional chief accountant				=SUM(B13:D13)
14	Assistant accountant				=SUM(B14:D14)
15	Accounting technician				=SUM(B15:D15)
16	Secretary				=SUM(B16:D16)
17	Total	=SUM(B13:B16)	=SUM(C13:C16)	=SUM(D13:D16)	=SUM(E13:E16)
18					
19	*Chargeout rates*				
20	Divisional chief accountant	72.5	=$B20	=$B20	
21	Assistant accountant	38	=$B21	=$B21	
22	Accounting technician	21.45	=$B22	=$B22	
23	Secretary	17.3	=$B23	=$B23	
24					

BPP PUBLISHING

(b) The final spreadsheet is as follows.

	A	B	C	D	E
1	**Special assignment**				
2	Personnel Costs				
3		**Week 1**	**Week 2**	**Week 3**	**Total**
4		Cost	Cost	Cost	Cost
5		£	£	£	£
6	Divisional chief accountant	0.00	326.25	489.38	815.63
7	Assistant accountant	760.00	1520.00	1330.00	3610.00
8	Accounting technician	686.40	858.00	804.38	2348.78
9	Secretary	259.50	556.54	644.43	1460.47
10	Total cost	1705.90	3260.79	3268.18	8234.87
11					
12		Hours	Hours	Hours	Hours
13	Divisional chief accountant	0.00	4.50	6.75	11.25
14	Assistant accountant	20.00	40.00	35.00	95.00
15	Accounting technician	32.00	40.00	37.50	109.50
16	Secretary	15.00	32.17	37.25	84.42
17	Total	67.00	116.67	116.50	300.17
18					
19	*Chargeout rates*				
20	Divisional chief accountant	72.50	72.50	72.50	
21	Assistant accountant	38.00	38.00	38.00	
22	Accounting technician	21.45	21.45	21.45	
23	Secretary	17.30	17.30	17.30	
24					

Solution to Activity 16

Before you can input any of the new data, you need to amend the design of the spreadsheet by inserting a column for week 4, altering your SUM formulae as necessary adding extra lines for the laptops and taking account of the chargeout rate change. (We have treated a laptop unit as a single 40-hour unit; you might have chosen to allocate 40 one-hour units to each.)

The revised spreadsheet before data entry is shown below. This is a very hard spreadsheet to alter especially if you set it up badly to start with.

	A	B	C	D	E	F
1	Special assignment					
2	Costs					
3		**Week 1**	**Week 2**	**Week 3**	**Week 4**	**Total**
4		Cost	Cost	Cost	Cost	Cost
5	*Personnel*	£	£	£	£	£
6	Divisional chief accountant	=B15*B25	=C15*C25	=D15*D25	=E15*E25	=SUM(B6:E6)
7	Assistant accountant	=B16*B26	=C16*C26	=D16*D26	=E16*E26	=SUM(B7:E7)
8	Accounting technician	=B17*B27	=C17*C27	=D17*D27	=E17*E27	=SUM(B8:E8)
9	Secretary	=B18*B28	=C18*C28	=D18*D28	=E18*E28	=SUM(B9:E9)
10	Total personnel cost	=SUM(B6:B9)	=SUM(C6:C9)	=SUM(D6:D9)		=SUM(F6:F9)
11	Cost of laptops	=B22*B29	=C22*C29	=D22*D29	=E22*E29	=SUM(B11:E11)
12	Total cost	=SUM(B6:B11)	=SUM(C6:C11)	=SUM(D6:D11)	=SUM(E6:E11)	=SUM(F10:F11)
13						
14	*Personnel*	Hours	Hours	Hours	Hours	Hours
15	Divisional chief accountant	0	4.5	6.75	6	=SUM(B15:E15)
16	Assistant accountant	20	40	35	0	=SUM(B16:E16)
17	Accounting technician	32	40	37.5	0	=SUM(B17:E17)
18	Secretary	15	32.17	37.25	0	=SUM(B18:E18)
19	Total	=SUM(B15:B18)	=SUM(C15:C18)	=SUM(D15:D18)	=SUM(E15:E18)	=SUM(F15:F18)
20						
21	*Laptops*	No	No	No	No	
22		2	2	2		
23						
24	*Chargeout rates*					
25	Divisional chief accountant	72.5	=$B25	=$B25	=$B25	
26	Assistant accountant	38	=$B26	=$B26	=$B26	
27	Accounting technician	21.45	=$B27	=$B27	=$B27	
28	Secretary	17.3	=$B28	=$B28*1.1	=$B28*1.1	
29	Laptops	100	=$B29	=$B29	=$B29	
30						
31						

The final spreadsheet is shown below.

	A	B	C	D	E	F
1	Special assignment					
2	Costs					
3		Week 1	Week 2	Week 3	Week 4	Total
4		Cost	Cost	Cost	Cost	Cost
5	*Personnel*	£	£	£	£	£
6	Divisional chief accountant	0.00	326.25	489.38	435.00	1250.63
7	Assistant accountant	760.00	1520.00	1330.00	0.00	3610.00
8	Accounting technician	686.40	858.00	804.38	0.00	2348.78
9	Secretary	259.50	556.54	708.87	0.00	1524.91
10	Total personnel cost	1705.9	3260.79	3332.62	435.00	8734.3085
11	Cost of laptops	200	200	200	0	600
12	Total cost	1905.90	3460.79	3532.62	435.00	9334.31
13						
14	*Personnel*	Hours	Hours	Hours	Hours	Hours
15	Divisional chief accountant	0.00	4.50	6.75	6.00	17.25
16	Assistant accountant	20.00	40.00	35.00	0.00	95.00
17	Accounting technician	32.00	40.00	37.50	0.00	109.50
18	Secretary	15.00	32.17	37.25	0.00	84.42
19	Total	67.00	116.67	116.50	6.00	306.17
20						
21	*Laptops*	No	No	No	No	
22		2	2	2	0	
23						

Solution to Activity 17

We adopted the following approach.

(a)   Inclusion of appropriate titles and column headings. We have included a 'Sundry' column for each of the payments *and* receipts.

(b)   Inclusion of additional columns for entry of narrative, date and reference of the user's choice (eg to show where the b/f entry comes from).

(c)   Once-only entry of each transaction in the appropriate analysed column. This is then *automatically* taken to the receipts or payments column as appropriate and then a new total inserted.

(d)   To prevent zeros being displayed all down columns E and H, we selected Tools and then Options and turned off the display of zero values.

(e)   To prevent totals being displayed all down column N, we used a conditional function to ensure that totals are only displayed as far down the page as the entries have been made. We have assumed that, because only a payment or a receipt is entered on a single line, if payments and receipts are equal, they must both equal zero and therefore have no entries. This will become clear if you try it out.

(f)   To prevent accidental or deliberate manipulation of the page, we selected Tools and then Protect Sheet, having first ensured that cell protection had been switched off (unlocked) for the following cells through the Format Cell..menu.

　　　　A9-B28
　　　　D9-D28
　　　　F9-G28
　　　　I9-M28
　　　　F2-F3

Our spreadsheet looks like this. The password to open the copy in the BPP data (**Ac_17_S**)is:

Enuff

	A	B	C	D	E	F	G	H	I	J	K	L	M	N
1	Bright Ideas Ltd													
2	Petty cash				Week number:									
3					Week ending:									
4														
5														
6	Narrative		Date	Line	Ref	Receipts	Sales	Sundry	Payments	Postage	Static	Kitch	Gifts	Sund Balance
7						£	£	£	£	£	£	£	£	£
8	Balance b/f													
9				1	=F9+G9			=SUM(I9:M9)						=IF(E9=H9,0,N8+E9-H9)
10				2	=F10+G10			=SUM(I10:M10)						=IF(E10=H10,0,N9+E10-H10)
11				3	=F11+G11			=SUM(I11:M11)						=IF(E11=H11,0,N10+E11-H11)
12				4	=F12+G12			=SUM(I12:M12)						=IF(E12=H12,0,N11+E12-H12)
13				5	=F13+G13			=SUM(I13:M13)						=IF(E13=H13,0,N12+E13-H13)
14				6	=F14+G14			=SUM(I14:M14)						=IF(E14=H14,0,N13+E14-H14)
15				7	=F15+G15			=SUM(I15:M15)						=IF(E15=H15,0,N14+E15-H15)
16				8	=F16+G16			=SUM(I16:M16)						=IF(E16=H16,0,N15+E16-H16)
17				9	=F17+G17			=SUM(I17:M17)						=IF(E17=H17,0,N16+E17-H17)
18				10	=F18+G18			=SUM(I18:M18)						=IF(E18=H18,0,N17+E18-H18)
19				11	=F19+G19			=SUM(I19:M19)						=IF(E19=H19,0,N18+E19-H19)
20				12	=F20+G20			=SUM(I20:M20)						=IF(E20=H20,0,N19+E20-H20)
21				13	=F21+G21			=SUM(I21:M21)						=IF(E21=H21,0,N20+E21-H21)
22				14	=F22+G22			=SUM(I22:M22)						=IF(E22=H22,0,N21+E22-H22)
23				15	=F23+G23			=SUM(I23:M23)						=IF(E23=H23,0,N22+E23-H23)
24				16	=F24+G24			=SUM(I24:M24)						=IF(E24=H24,0,N23+E24-H24)
25				17	=F25+G25			=SUM(I25:M25)						=IF(E25=H25,0,N24+E25-H25)
26				18	=F26+G26			=SUM(I26:M26)						=IF(E26=H26,0,N25+E26-H26)
27				19	=F27+G27			=SUM(I27:M27)						=IF(E27=H27,0,N26+E27-H27)
28				20	=F28+G28			=SUM(I28:M28)						=IF(E28=H28,0,N27+E28-H28)
29	Total				=SUM(E9:E28)	=SUM(F9:F28)	=SUM(G9:G28)	=SUM(H9:H28)	=SUM(I9:I28)	=SUM	=SUM	=SUM	=SUM	=N8+E29-H29
30														

We could have added further features as follows, but we decided that, as this is petty cash, we had probably done enough! You may well have thought of these or others of your own.

(a)   Conditional functions to ensure that each line is used in turn.

(b)   Conditional function to cross check the contents of cell N29.

(c)   Linked worksheets to ensure that totals are automatically carried forward to the following week.

(d)   Formulae to calculate the amount to be banked or the cheque required to be cashed.

Solution to Activity 18

The completed spreadsheet is shown below. You should note the following.

(a)   We have ignored the IOU, treating it as cash. Of course, such practices as writing IOUs should be discouraged from the control point of view.

(b)   We have formatted the spreadsheet to display two decimal places.

(c)   The formula in cell G22 is =N8-N21. We could have set up separate columns for bank receipts and bank payments.

(d)   Most spreadsheet packages offer a choice of display formats for dates. We selected the B column and clicked on it with the right mouse button to format the cells. The result is that whatever format we *enter* a date in (eg 8/9), it will be displayed as specified (eg 8-Sep).

	A	B	C	D	E	F	G	H	I	J	K	L	M	N
1	Bright Ideas Ltd													
2	Petty cash				Week number:									
3					Week ending:									
4														
5														
6	Narrative	Date	Line	Ref	Receipts	Sales	Sundry	Payments	Postage	Stationery	Kitchen	Gifts	Sundry	Balance
7					£	£	£	£	£	£	£	£	£	£
8	Balance b/f													250.00
9	Cash sale	08-Sep	1	2388	25.60	25.60								275.60
10	Cash sale	08-Sep	2	2389	13.55	13.55								289.15
11	Coffee	08-Sep	3	4998				12.96			12.96			276.19
12	Cash sale	09-Sep	4	2390	25.60	25.60								301.79
13	Envelopes	09-Sep	5	4999				3.95		3.95				297.84
14	Stamps	09-Sep	6	4000				25.00	25.00					272.84
15	Cash sale	10-Sep	7	2391	4.00	4.00								276.84
16	Cash sale	10-Sep	8	2392	13.55	13.55								290.39
17	Wedding gift AF	10-Sep	9	4001				74.99				74.99		215.40
18	Taxi	11-Sep	10	4002				8.00					8.00	207.40
19	Cash sale	12-Sep	11	2393	12.00	12.00								219.40
20	Christian Aid	12-Sep	12	4003				20.00					20.00	199.40
21	Speedpost	12-Sep	13	4004				32.71	32.71					166.69
22	Cheque	12-Sep	14	Bank	83.31		83.31							250.00
23			15											
24			16											
25			17											
26			18											
27			19											
28			20											
29	Total				177.61	94.30	83.31	177.61	57.71	3.95	12.96	74.99	28.00	250.00
30														

Solution to Activity 19

The completed job cost cards are shown below. There are many different ways of setting up this data: this is only one suggestion because there is not necessarily a   best answer without more information.

Note the following.

(a)   We have assumed that damaged stock cannot be identified with any particular job.

(b)   Actual overhead costs are irrelevant; it is the recovery percentages which are important here.

(c)   The spreadsheet has been designed to enable it to be used in other periods with other jobs. If you are not sure about this, try copying the formulae and format across to create a new column (or, in our example, 2 columns) to the right of the existing spreadsheet. If you enter data in rows 8-10 and 13-17 only, a new job cost card should be calculated below.

Linked three-dimensional sheets (one per month) could be constructed too.

	A	B	C	D	E
1	**Bodger & Co**				
2	Summarised job cards				
3	September 20X5				
4					
5	*Costs b/f*				
6			*Job no. 487*		*Job no. 488*
7		Hours	£	Hours	£
8	Direct materials		1025.00		
9	Direct labour	120	525.00		
10	Production overhead		360.00		
11			1910.00		
12	*September*				
13	Direct materials		3585.00		5850.00
14	Material transfers		-1125.00		1125.00
15	Returns to stores		-1305.00		
16	Direct labour	445	2002.50	280	1260.00
17	Invoice value		8050.00		12000.00
18					
19	*Data table*	£			
20	Labour cost per hour	4.50			
21	Production o'head rate	3.00			
22	Admin/mkting o'head rate	0.2			
23					
24					
25	**Summarised job cost cards**				
26			*Job no. 487*		*Job no. 488*
27	Direct materials		2180.00		6975.00
28	Direct labour		2527.50		1260.00
29	Production overhead		1695.00		840.00
30	Factory cost		6402.50		9075.00
31	Admin/mkting o'head		1280.50		1815.00
32	Cost of sale		7683.00		10890.00
33	Invoice value		8050.00		12000.00
34	Profit/loss on job		367.00		1110.00
35					

The formulae we have used are as follows. This file is available in the BPP data as **Ac_19_S**. The password is **JobNos**

	A	B	C	D	E
1	**Bodger & Co**				
2	Summarised job cards				
3	September 20X5				
4					
5	*Costs b/f*				
6			*Job no. 487*		*Job no. 488*
7		Hours	£	Hours	£
8	Direct materials		1025		0
9	Direct labour	120	525		0
10	Production overhead		=B9*$B$21		=D9*$B$21
11			=SUM(C8:C10)		=SUM(E8:E10)
12	*September*				
13	Direct materials		3585		5850
14	Material transfers		-1125		1125
15	Returns to stores		-1305		0
16	Direct labour	445	=B16*$B$20	280	=D16*$B$20
17	Invoice value		8050		12000
18					
19	*Data table*	£			
20	Labour cost per hour	4.5			
21	Production o'head rate	3			
22	Admin/mkting o'head rate	0.2			
23					
24					
25	**Summarised job cost cards**				
26			*Job no. 487*		*Job no. 488*
27	Direct materials		=C8+C13+C14+C15		=E8+E13+E14+E15
28	Direct labour		=C9+C16		=E9+E16
29	Production overhead		=+C10+B16*$B$21		=+E10+D16*$B$21
30	Factory cost		=SUM(C27:C29)		=SUM(E27:E29)
31	Admin/mkting o'head		=C30*$B$22		=E30*$B$22
32	Cost of sale		=SUM(C30:C31)		=SUM(E30:E31)
33	Invoice value		=C17		=E17
34	Profit/loss on job		=C33-C32		=E33-E32

Solution to Activity 20

The final ETB is shown below. You should have spotted that the 'bank' figure is an overdraft - otherwise your opening TB columns would not have balanced.

	A	B	C	D	E	F	G	H	I	J	K	L
1	Vincent											
2	ETB Year Ended 31/12/X7											
3	Account		Trial balance		Adjustments		Accrued	Prepaid	Profit and loss		Balance sheet	
4			£	£	£	£	£	£	£	£	£	£
5												
6	F & F cost	B	21,650								21,650	
7	F & F depn	B		(12,965)		(3,954)						(16,919)
8	MV cost	B	37,628								37,628	
9	MV depn	B		(17,490)		(8,643)						(26,133)
10	Stock at 01 Jan 20X7	P	34,285						34,285			
11	Sales ledger control	B	91,440		4,300	(2,440)					93,300	
12	Doubtful debt provision	B		(3,409)		(1,256)						(4,665)
13	Cash	B	361								361	
14	Bank	B		(14,297)								(14,297)
15	Purch ledger control	B		(102,157)								(102,157)
16	Sales	P		(354,291)		(4,300)				(358,591)		
17	Purchases	P	197,981						197,981			
18	Wages and salaries	P	57,980						57,980			
19	Rent and rates	P	31,650				6,750		38,400			
20	Advertising	P	12,240					(1,500)	10,740			
21	Administrative expenses	P	31,498						31,498			
22	Bank charges	P	2,133				508		2,641			
23	Bad debts written off	P	763		3,696				4,459			
24	Capital	B		(15,000)		(10,000)						(25,000)
25	Stock at 31 Dec 20X7	B			37,238						37,238	
26	Stock at 31 Dec 20X7	P				(37,238)				(37,238)		
27	Accruals	B					(7,258)					(7,258)
28	Prepayments	B						1,500			1,500	
29	Depreciation expense	P			12,597				12,597			
30	Sundry debtors	B			10,000						10,000	
31												
32												
33	SUB-TOTAL		519,609	(519,609)	67,831	(67,831)	8,758	(8,758)	390,581	(395,829)	201,677	(196,429)
34	Profit for the year								5,248			(5,248)
35	TOTAL		519,609	(519,609)	67,831	(67,831)	8,758	(8,758)	395,829	(395,829)	201,677	(201,677)

Adjustments and formulae used (besides the standard ETB ones) are shown on the next page. The adjustments regarding depreciation and the effect on the provision for bad debts of late sales required some careful thought.

	A	B	C	D	E
37					
38	**Adjustments**				
39	*Depreciation*				
40	MV		8643		
41	FF		3954		
42	Depreciation expense			12597	
43					
44	*Bad debts*				
45	Debtors		93,300		
46	Provision %		5%		
47	New provision		4665		
48	Current provision		-3,409		
49	Increase			1256	
50	Bad Debts		2440		
51				2440	
52				3696	
53					
54	*Stock*				
55	Closing stock		37238		
56					
57	**Accruals**				
58	Bank charges		508		
59	Rent		6750		
60				7258	
61					
62	**Prepayments**				
63					
64	Advertising		1500		
65				1500	
66					
67	**Sales**				
68	Post Xmas		4300		
69					
70	**Capital**				
71	New capital		10000		
72					

	A	B	C	D	E
37					
38	**Adjustments**				
39	*Depreciation*				
40	MV		=1146+((C8-7640)*0.25)		
41	FF		=(C6-1880)*0.2		
42	Depreciation expense			=SUM(C40:C41)	
43					
44	*Bad debts*				
45	Debtors		=(C11+C68)-2440		
46	Provision %		0.05		
47	New provision		=C46*C45		
48	Current provision		=D12		
49	Increase			=SUM(C47:C48)	
50	Bad Debts		2440		
51				=SUM(C49:C50)	
52				=SUM(D49:D51)	
53					
54	*Stock*				
55	Closing stock		37238		
56					
57	**Accruals**				
58	Bank charges		508		
59	Rent		6750		
60				=SUM(C58:C59)	
61					
62	**Prepayments**				
63					
64	Advertising		1500		
65				=SUM(C63:C64)	
66					
67	**Sales**				
68	Post Xmas		4300		
69					
70	**Capital**				
71	New capital		10000		
72					

Solution to Activity 21

The final spreadsheet is shown below and is available as **Ac_21_S** in the BPP data. The password is **Old1**

	A	B	C	D	E	F	G	H	I	J	K	L	M	N	O	P
1	Dittori Sage Ltd															
2	Debtors ageing by region															
3	Date - 31 May 20X6															
4																
5	Region	Balance	Current	1 month	2 month	3 month	4 month	5 month +		Curr	1 mth	2 mth	3 mth	4 mth	5 mth+	Total
6		£	£	£	£	£	£	£								
7	Highlands	1,001.41	346.60	567.84	32.17			54.80		34.6%	56.7%	3.2%			5.5%	100%
8	Strathclyde	59,578.78	24,512.05	28,235.50	4,592.50	1,244.80	51.36	942.57		41.1%	47.4%	7.7%	2.1%	0.1%	1.6%	100%
9	Borders	2,440.65	1,927.77		512.88					79.0%		21.0%				100%
10	North West	18,249.10	824.80	14,388.91	2,473.53		482.20	79.66		4.5%	78.8%	13.6%		2.6%	0.4%	100%
11	North East	32,243.59	14,377.20	12,850.00		3,771.84	1,244.55			44.6%	39.9%		11.7%	3.9%		100%
12	Midlands	140,737.86	45,388.27	61,337.88	24,001.02	4,288.31	1,391.27	4,331.11		32.3%	43.6%	17.1%	3.0%	1.0%	3.1%	100%
13	Wales	25,630.84	14,318.91	5,473.53	21.99	4,881.64	512.27	422.50		55.9%	21.4%	0.1%	19.0%	2.0%	1.6%	100%
14	East Anglia	3,242.14	157.20	943.68	377.40	1,500.87	15.33	247.66		4.8%	29.1%	11.6%	46.3%	0.5%	7.6%	100%
15	South West	32,735.50	9,528.73	11,983.39	3,771.89	6,228.77	1,008.21	214.51		29.1%	36.6%	11.5%	19.0%	3.1%	0.7%	100%
16	South East	225,179.78	68,110.78	83,914.54	29,117.96	24,285.10	14,328.90	5,422.50		30.2%	37.3%	12.9%	10.8%	6.4%	2.4%	100%
17	France	25,244.78	6,422.80	7,451.47	5,897.55	2,103.70	140.50	3,228.76		25.4%	29.5%	23.4%	8.3%	0.6%	12.8%	100%
18	Other EU	22,669.00	5,433.88	4,991.90	5,012.70	4,223.80	1,022.43	1,984.29		24.0%	22.0%	22.1%	18.6%	4.5%	8.8%	100%
19	Rest of world	10,121.21	1,822.70	4,529.67	277.50	3,491.34				18.0%	44.8%	2.7%	34.5%			100%
20	Total	599,074.64	193,171.69	236,668.31	76,089.09	56,020.17	20,197.02	16,928.36		32.2%	39.5%	12.7%	9.4%	3.4%	2.8%	100%

Formulae used are as follows (selected columns only: look at the file itself for the full formulae). Note the use of the absolute address in cell J7 to facilitate copying across and down. Column P is optional. Columns J to P can be formatted in % style.

	A	B	C	I	J	K	L	M	N	O	P
1	Dittori Sage Ltd										
2	Debtors ageing by region										
3	Date - 31 May 20X6										
4											
5	Region	Balance	Current		Curr	1 mth	2 mth	3 mth	4 mth	5 mth+	Total
6		£	£								
7	Highlands	=SUM(C7:H7)	346.6		=C7/$B7	=D7/$B7	=E7/$B7	=F7/$B7	=G7/$B7	=H7/$B7	=SUM(J7:O7)
8	Strathclyde	=SUM(C8:H8)	24512.05		=C8/$B8	=D8/$B8	=E8/$B8	=F8/$B8	=G8/$B8	=H8/$B8	=SUM(J8:O8)
9	Borders	=SUM(C9:H9)	1927.77		=C9/$B9	=D9/$B9	=E9/$B9	=F9/$B9	=G9/$B9	=H9/$B9	=SUM(J9:O9)
10	North West	=SUM(C10:H10)	824.8		=C10/$B10	=D10/$B10	=E10/$B10	=F10/$B10	=G10/$B10	=H10/$B10	=SUM(J10:O10)
11	North East	=SUM(C11:H11)	14377.2		=C11/$B11	=D11/$B11	=E11/$B11	=F11/$B11	=G11/$B11	=H11/$B11	=SUM(J11:O11)
12	Midlands	=SUM(C12:H12)	45388.27		=C12/$B12	=D12/$B12	=E12/$B12	=F12/$B12	=G12/$B12	=H12/$B12	=SUM(J12:O12)
13	Wales	=SUM(C13:H13)	14318.91		=C13/$B13	=D13/$B13	=E13/$B13	=F13/$B13	=G13/$B13	=H13/$B13	=SUM(J13:O13)
14	East Anglia	=SUM(C14:H14)	157.2		=C14/$B14	=D14/$B14	=E14/$B14	=F14/$B14	=G14/$B14	=H14/$B14	=SUM(J14:O14)
15	South West	=SUM(C15:H15)	9528.73		=C15/$B15	=D15/$B15	=E15/$B15	=F15/$B15	=G15/$B15	=H15/$B15	=SUM(J15:O15)
16	South East	=SUM(C16:H16)	68110.78		=C16/$B16	=D16/$B16	=E16/$B16	=F16/$B16	=G16/$B16	=H16/$B16	=SUM(J16:O16)
17	France	=SUM(C17:H17)	6422.8		=C17/$B17	=D17/$B17	=E17/$B17	=F17/$B17	=G17/$B17	=H17/$B17	=SUM(J17:O17)
18	Other EU	=SUM(C18:H18)	5433.88		=C18/$B18	=D18/$B18	=E18/$B18	=F18/$B18	=G18/$B18	=H18/$B18	=SUM(J18:O18)
19	Rest of world	=SUM(C19:H19)	1822.7		=C19/$B19	=D19/$B19	=E19/$B19	=F19/$B19	=G19/$B19	=H19/$B19	=SUM(J19:O19)
20	Total	=SUM(B7:B19)	=SUM(C7:C19)		=C20/$B20	=D20/$B20	=E20/$B20	=F20/$B20	=G20/$B20	=H20/$B20	=SUM(J20:O20)

Solution to Activity 22

You should have creates a spreadsheet to calculate NPV at 10% and then simply changed the Interest rate variable to do the second part of the question.

NPV at 10%	£12,030	The project should be accepted because it gives a positive NPV
NPV at 11%	(£48,020	The project should be rejected because it gives a negative NPV

The IRR is clearly between 10% and 11%. It works out at 10.1926%.

Here is the spreadsheet used to calculate these figures. You can have a closer look by opening the file **Ac_22_S** in the BPP data (password: **Xmas**).

	A	B	C	D	E	F
1	**NPV calculation**				**IRR calculation**	
2		£'000	£'000			£'000
3	Costs incurred now		-1500.00		Costs incurred now	-1500.00
4	Savings year 1	271.00			Savings year 1	271.00
5	Savings year 2	226.00			Savings year 2	226.00
6	Savings year 3	249.00			Savings year 3	249.00
7	Savings year 4	275.00			Savings year 4	275.00
8	Savings year 5	265.00			Savings year 5	265.00
9	Savings year 6	300.00			Savings year 6	300.00
10	Savings year 7	177.00			Savings year 7	177.00
11	Savings year 8	205.00			Savings year 8	205.00
12	Savings year 9	223.00			Savings year 9	223.00
13	Savings year 10	231.00			Savings year 10	231.00
14	Discounted value		1451.18			
15	**Net present value**		-48.82		**IRR**	10.1926%
16						
17						
18						
19	**Rate**	11%				
20						

The formulae are as follows.

	A	B	C	D	E	F
1	**NPV calculation**				**IRR calculation**	
2		£'000	£'000			£'000
3	Costs incurred now		-1500		Costs incurred now	-1500
4	Savings year 1	271			Savings year 1	271
5	Savings year 2	226			Savings year 2	226
6	Savings year 3	249			Savings year 3	249
7	Savings year 4	275			Savings year 4	275
8	Savings year 5	265			Savings year 5	265
9	Savings year 6	300			Savings year 6	300
10	Savings year 7	177			Savings year 7	177
11	Savings year 8	205			Savings year 8	205
12	Savings year 9	223			Savings year 9	223
13	Savings year 10	231			Savings year 10	231
14	Discounted value		=NPV(B19,B4:B13)			
15	**Net present value**		=SUM(C3:C14)		IRR	=IRR(F3:F13)
16						
17						
18						
19	**Rate**	0.1				
20						

Solution to Activity 23

If you tried doing a simple Sort you would have got nowhere with this because data is sorted left to right. What you need to be able to do is separate out the alphabetical information from the numerical information.

Fortunately there is a useful function in Excel that allows you to do this.

In the solution shown below the formula in column B **=RIGHT(A1,2)** extracts the two rightmost characters from the entry in column A, while the formula in column C **=LEFT(A1,4)** extracts the four leftmost characters.

The data as a whole (including the data in column A) can then be sorted by column B then by column C to give the results shown below for the first few rows.

	A	B	C
1	4842AA	AA	4842
2	5736AA	AA	5736
3	8162AA	AA	8162
4	7635AB	AB	7635
5	7880AB	AB	7880
6	8884AB	AB	8884
7	6856AC	AC	6856
8	6851AD	AD	6851
9	3320AE	AE	3320
10	3635AE	AE	3635
11	5571AF	AF	5571
12	8406AF	AF	8406
13	6139AG	AG	6139
14	6305AG	AG	6305
15	8282AG	AG	8282
16	1118AI	AI	1118
17	9581AI	AI	9581
18	7540AJ	AJ	7540
19	7733AJ	AJ	7733
20	3679AK	AK	3679
21	9337AK	AK	9337
22	5929AL	AL	5929
23	6171AL	AL	6171
24	6248AL	AL	6248
25	8507AL	AL	8507

The full answer is provided in the BPP file **Ac_23_S** for which the password is **HANDY**

The question of duplicates is dealt with in columns D and E of our answer. Once you have sorted the data you can do a simple test to see if the entry in one row equal to the entry in the previous row, and return 1 if so, 0 if not: **=IF(A2=A1,1,0)**. You then sum the column in which your 1's and 0s are returned. This saves you having to look right through 1500 records. If it sums to more than 0 you know there is a duplicate entry.

To find it quickly, copy the column with the duplicate-finding formulae into the next column as a **number** (in Excel, **Edit … Paste Special … Values**) and then do a computer search (**Edit Find**) just on row E, for the number 1.

You should have found one duplicate: the item coded **1005FL** appears twice.

Solution to Activity 24

The file **Ac_24_S** shows you how this is done. You should be experienced enough by now to be able to explore the spreadsheet yourself to see how it has been constructed.

The password for this file is **nestedifelse**

Solution to Activity 25

The file **PCPlod_S** (in C:\BPPU21\Access) includes the two queries you should have built.

The password for this file is **oldbill**

Solutions to Practice Devolved Assessments

SOLUTION TO PRACTICE DEVOLVED ASSESSMENT 1: BROOM RIGGS

Parts of the solution are available in the BPP file **DA1_S.** The password to open this is:

MrsPeel

(a)   No written solution given.

(b)   See the next page.

(c)   You should know how to use whatever anti-virus measures are installed on your PC. You may have a proprietary package such as Dr Solomon's Anti-Virus Toolkit or Norton Anti-Virus.

(d)   Start up Explorer, click on '3^1/$_2$ Floppy' or 'A', click on File, then New, then Folder.

(e)   This can be done using the File Delete commands in Windows Explorer. Colleges usually do not allow students to have access to hard disks, so you may well not have made a hard disk copy to start with.

(f)   No written solution.

(g)   To set a 3½ floppy disk to write protect, you should slide the plastic tab to leave the hole visible.

Suitable storage might be any purpose-built disk storage, probably a lockable plastic filing tray or storage racks in a cupboard or drawer.

BPP PUBLISHING

	Microsoft Excel					_□×
	File Edit View Insert Format Tools Data Window Help					

	A	B	C	D	E	F
1		**Broom Riggs Ltd**				
2		**Extended trial balance**				
3		*Year ended 31 December 20X8*				
5		**Account**		**Trial balance**		
6				£	£	
7	A1	Accountancy fees	P	440.00		
8	A2	Advertising	P	1,556.29		
9	B1	Bank account	B		(27,488.12)	
10	B2	Bank charges	P	2,157.51		
11	B3	Bank interest	P	1,109.11		
12	B4	Bad debt expense	P			
13	C1	Credit card charges	P	2,212.80		
14	D1	Discounts allowed	P	5,629.31		
15	D2	Discounts received	P		(4,529.69)	
16	D3	Directors' loan accounts	B	9,343.89		
17	D4F	Depreciation: fixtures and fittin	B		(14,304.00)	
18	D4N	Depreciation: motor vehicles	B		(22,563.10)	
19	D4L	Depreciation: leasehold	B		(38,500.00)	
20	D5	Depreciation expense	P			
21	D6	Doubtful debt provision	B			
22	E1	Electricity	P	7,264.61		
23	F1	Fixtures and fittings	B	35,430.00		
24	G1	Gas	P	12,374.97		
25	I1	Insurance	P	22,298.96		
26	L1	Leasehold	B	220,000.00		
27	L2	Loan	B		(50,000.00)	
28	L3	Loan interest	P	5,000.00		
29	M1	Maintenance	P	4,649.22		
30	M2	Motor expenses	P	1,557.10		
31	M3	Motor vehicles	B	73,482.10		
32	P1	Profit and loss account	B		(160,808.95)	
33	P2	Purchases	P	499,227.91		
34	P3	Purchase ledger control accoul	B		(51,444.74)	
35	P4	Petty cash	B	1,000.00		
36	P5	Purchase returns	P		(687.08)	
37	P6	Print, post and stationery	P	5,885.32		
38	P7	PAYE and NI	P	91,799.27		
39	R1	Rates	P	30,616.08		
40	R2	Rent (warehouse)	P	18,125.00		
41	S1	Share capital	B		(100,000.00)	
42	S2	Sales	P		(1,022,734.87)	
43	S3	Sales ledger control account	B	105,947.07		
44	S4	Sales returns	P	2,287.03		
45	S5	Staff welfare	P	1,768.56		
46	S6	Stock at 1 January 20X8	P	48,172.29		
47	S7	Sundry expenses	P	1,574.68		
48	T1	Telephone	P	8,763.82		
49	V1	VAT	B		(18,965.89)	
50	W1	Wages and salaries	P	266,449.27		
51	W2	Water rates	P	9,454.27		
52	X1	Suspense account	B	16,450.00		
53	-	Closing stock	P			
54	-	Closing stock	B			
55	-	Accruals	B			
56	-	Prepayments	B			
58		SUB-TOTAL		1,512,026.44	(1,512,026.44)	
59		Profit for the year				
60		**TOTAL**		1,512,026.44	(1,512,026.44)	
61						

| | | | | NUM | | |

(h)   We did calculations on a separate sheet as follows. The formulae used are also shown.

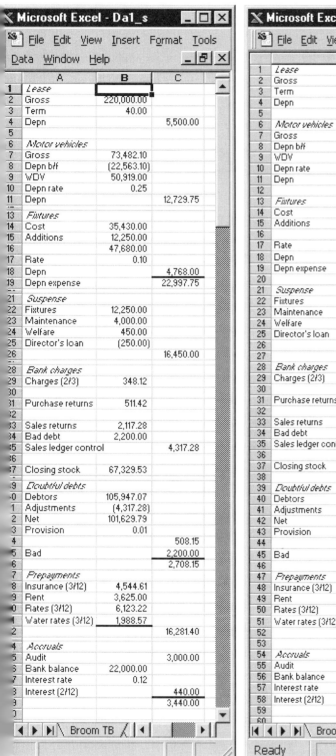

	A	B	C
1	*Lease*		
2	Gross	220,000.00	
3	Term	40.00	
4	Depn		5,500.00
5			
6	*Motor vehicles*		
7	Gross	73,482.10	
8	Depn b/f	(22,563.10)	
9	WDV	50,919.00	
10	Depn rate	0.25	
11	Depn		12,729.75
13	*Fixtures*		
14	Cost	35,430.00	
15	Additions	12,250.00	
16		47,680.00	
17	Rate	0.10	
18	Depn		4,768.00
19	Depn expense		22,997.75
21	*Suspense*		
22	Fixtures	12,250.00	
23	Maintenance	4,000.00	
24	Welfare	450.00	
25	Director's loan	(250.00)	
26			16,450.00
28	*Bank charges*		
29	Charges (2/3)	348.12	
31	Purchase returns	511.42	
33	Sales returns	2,117.28	
34	Bad debt	2,200.00	
35	Sales ledger control		4,317.28
37	Closing stock	67,329.53	
39	*Doubtful debts*		
40	Debtors	105,947.07	
41	Adjustments	(4,317.28)	
42	Net	101,629.79	
43	Provision	0.01	
44			508.15
45	Bad		2,200.00
46			2,708.15
47	*Prepayments*		
48	Insurance (3/12)	4,544.61	
49	Rent	3,625.00	
50	Rates (3/12)	6,123.22	
51	Water rates (3/12)	1,988.57	
52			16,281.40
54	*Accruals*		
55	Audit		3,000.00
56	Bank balance	22,000.00	
57	Interest rate	0.12	
58	Interest (2/12)		440.00
59			3,440.00

| | Broom TB |

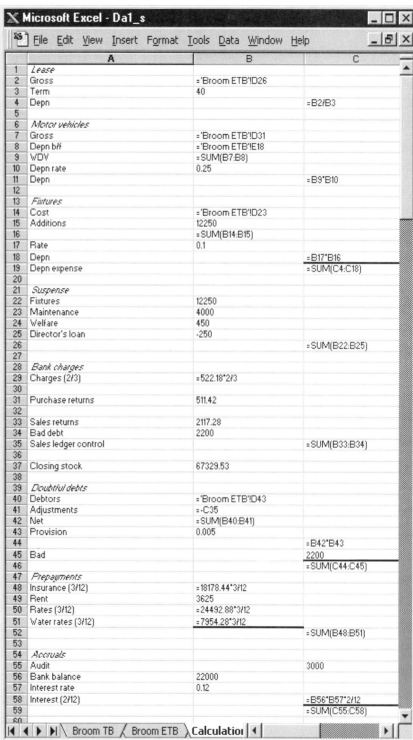

	A	B	C
1	*Lease*		
2	Gross	='Broom ETB'!D26	
3	Term	40	
4	Depn		=B2/B3
5			
6	*Motor vehicles*		
7	Gross	='Broom ETB'!D31	
8	Depn b/f	='Broom ETB'!E18	
9	WDV	=SUM(B7:B8)	
10	Depn rate	0.25	
11	Depn		=B9*B10
12			
13	*Fixtures*		
14	Cost	='Broom ETB'!D23	
15	Additions	12250	
16		=SUM(B14:B15)	
17	Rate	0.1	
18	Depn		=B17*B16
19	Depn expense		=SUM(C4:C18)
20			
21	*Suspense*		
22	Fixtures	12250	
23	Maintenance	4000	
24	Welfare	450	
25	Director's loan	-250	
26			=SUM(B22:B25)
27			
28	*Bank charges*		
29	Charges (2/3)	=522.18*2/3	
30			
31	Purchase returns	511.42	
32			
33	Sales returns	2117.28	
34	Bad debt	2200	
35	Sales ledger control		=SUM(B33:B34)
36			
37	Closing stock	67329.53	
38			
39	*Doubtful debts*		
40	Debtors	='Broom ETB'!D43	
41	Adjustments	=-C35	
42	Net	=SUM(B40:B41)	
43	Provision	0.005	
44			=B42*B43
45	Bad	2200	
46			=SUM(C44:C45)
47	*Prepayments*		
48	Insurance (3/12)	=18178.44*3/12	
49	Rent	3625	
50	Rates (3/12)	=24492.88*3/12	
51	Water rates (3/12)	=7954.28*3/12	
52			=SUM(B48:B51)
53			
54	*Accruals*		
55	Audit		3000
56	Bank balance	22000	
57	Interest rate	0.12	
58	Interest (2/12)		=B56*B57*2/12
59			=SUM(C55:C58)

| | Broom TB | Broom ETB | Calculation |

Ready   NUM

Practice devolved assessments

(i) As you already have an early copy of the ETB on your floppy disk (from part (d)), you should now have saved it under a different name.

(j)

Bream Rigg Ltd
Extended trial balance

Account		Trial balance Dr £	Trial balance Cr £	Adjustments Dr £	Adjustments Cr £	Accrued £	Prepaid £	Profit and loss Dr £	Profit and loss Cr £	Balance sheet Dr £	Balance sheet Cr £
A1 Accountancy fees	P	440.00				3,000.00		3,440.00			
A2 Advertising	P	1,556.29						1,556.29			
B1 Bank account	B		(27,488.12)		(348.12)						(27,836.24)
B2 Bank charges	P	2,157.51		348.12				2,505.63			
B3 Bank interest	P	1,109.11				440.00		1,549.11			
B4 Bad debt expense	P			2,708.15				2,708.15			
C1 Credit card charges	P	2,212.80						2,212.80			
D1 Discount allowed	P	5,629.31						5,629.31			
D2 Discount received	P		(4,529.69)						(4,529.69)		
D3 Directors' loan account	B	9,343.89			(250.00)					9,093.89	
D4F Depreciation: fixtures and fitti	B		(14,304.00)		(4,768.00)						(19,072.00)
D4M Depreciation: motor vehicles	B		(22,563.10)		(12,729.75)						(35,292.85)
D4L Depreciation: leasehold	B		(38,500.00)		(5,500.00)						(44,000.00)
D5 Depreciation expense	P			22,997.75				22,997.75			
D6 Doubtful debt provision	B				(508.15)						(508.15)
E1 Electricity	P	7,264.61						7,264.61			
F1 Fixtures and fitting	B	35,430.00		12,250.00						47,680.00	
G1 Gas	P	12,374.97						12,374.97			
I1 Insurance	P	22,298.96					(4,544.61)	17,754.35			
L1 Leasehold	B	220,000.00								220,000.00	
L2 Loan	B		(50,000.00)								(50,000.00)
L3 Loan interest	P	5,000.00						5,000.00			
M1 Maintenance	P	4,649.22		4,000.00				8,649.22			
M2 Motor expenses	P	1,557.10						1,557.10			
M3 Motor vehicles	B	73,482.10								73,482.10	
P1 Profit and loss account	B		(160,808.95)								(160,808.95)
P2 Purchases	P	499,227.91						499,227.91			
P3 Purchase ledger control accou	B		(51,444.74)	511.42							(50,933.32)
P4 Petty cash	B	1,000.00								1,000.00	
P5 Purchase returns	P		(687.08)		(511.42)				(1,198.50)		
P6 Print, part and stationery	P	5,885.32						5,885.32			
P7 PAYE and NI	P	91,799.27						91,799.27			
R1 Rates	P	30,616.08					(6,123.22)	24,492.86			
R2 Rent (warehouse)	P	18,125.00					(3,625.00)	14,500.00			
S1 Share capital	B		(100,000.00)								(100,000.00)
S2 Sales	P		(1,022,734.87)						(1,022,734.87)		
S3 Sales ledger control account	B	105,947.07			(4,317.28)					101,629.79	
S4 Sales returns	P	2,287.03		2,117.28				4,404.31			
S5 Staff welfare	P	1,768.56		450.00				2,218.56			
S6 Stock at 1 January 19XX	P	48,172.29						48,172.29			
S7 Sundry expenses	P	1,574.68						1,574.68			
T1 Telephone	P	8,763.82						8,763.82			
V1 VAT	B		(18,965.89)								(18,965.89)
W1 Wages and salaries	P	266,449.27						266,449.27			
W2 Water rates	P	9,454.27					(1,988.57)	7,465.70			
X1 Suspense account	P	16,450.00			(16,450.00)						
— Closing stock	B			67,329.53	(67,329.53)				(67,329.53)	63,889.53	
— Accruals	B					16,281.40				16,281.40	
— Prepayments	B						(3,440.00)				
SUB-TOTAL		1,512,026.44	(1,512,026.44)	112,712.25	(112,712.25)	19,721.40	(19,721.40)	1,070,153.28	(1,095,792.59)	533,056.71	(507,417.40)
Profit for the year								25,639.31			(25,639.31)
TOTAL		1,512,026.44	(1,512,026.44)	112,712.25	(112,712.25)	19,721.40	(19,721.40)	1,095,792.59	(1,095,792.59)	533,056.71	(533,056.71)

SOLUTION TO PRACTICE DEVOLVED ASSESSMENT 2: WILD THYME

Parts of the solution are available in the BPP file **DA2_S.** The password to open this is:

parsley

(a)   This spreadsheet should include the departmental statistics provided in the question and also data relating to the allocation of overheads. This is shown in lines 1-31 of the solution to part (f).

(b)   No written solution given.

(c)   Assuming that there is no network or electronic mail system, and that you therefore have to send the disk itself through the internal mail, you should consider the appropriateness of the following.

    (i)   Ensure that you have retained a back-up of the disk.

    (ii)   Use a proper package designed for the purpose, such as a cardboard wallet or a plastic disk wallet.

    (iii)   Identify clearly on the outside of the package that a disk is enclosed.

    (iv)   Mark the package 'private and confidential'.

    (v)   Consider using password protection on the spreadsheet so that it cannot be opened or accessed. This can be done in by selecting File Save As and then Options. You can then telephone your colleague separately to inform him of the password.

    (vi)   Address the package carefully, so that the risk of its going astray is minimised.

    (vii)   Do not use a standard internal mail brown envelope, as the disk might fall out. A padded envelope might be suitable.

(d)   This could be done using Windows Explorer.

(e)   If you realised that you did not mean to delete the file from the floppy, take the floppy out of the drive and write protect it. Do not save any more files to the disk. If you are sure that you know what to do, you could recover the File yourself using a proprietary package (eg Norton) or using the Undelete utility supplied with Windows. If you are not sure, then keep the disk safe and identify someone who can help.

(f)

	A	B	C	D	E	F	G
1	**Wild Thyme Ltd**						
2	**Overhead apportionment**						
3	**Budgeted figures**						
4	**Year ending 31 December 20X7**						
8	**Departmental statistics**						
9		**Dept C**	**Dept F**	**Dept A**	**Dept M**	**Dept R**	
10	Floor area (sq. m)	3,000	1,750	1,500	800	600	
11	Plant value	£32,000	£20,000	£16,000	£8,000	£4,000	
12	Hourly labour rate	£4.10	£5.14	£4.25	£4.00	£3.20	
13	Direct labour hours	4,200	1,200	2,000	-	-	
16	**Departmental overheads**						
17		*Totals*					
18		£					
19	Rent and rates	62,730					
20	Machine insurance	8,350					
21	Depreciation	16,450					
22	Production supervisor	24,300					
23	Heat and light	8,800					
24		120,630					
25							
26							
27	**Allocated overheads**						
28		**Dept C**	**Dept F**	**Dept A**	**Dept M**	**Dept R**	
29	Specific to department	£4,800	£2,200	£3,500	£2,000	£1,600	
30	Dept M	20%	58%	22%			
31	Dept R	55%	18%	27%			
34	**Apportionment calculation**						
35							
36		**Dept C**	**Dept F**	**Dept A**	**Dept M**	**Dept R**	**Total**
37	Costs specific to department	4,800.00	2,200.00	3,500.00	2,000.00	1,600.00	14,100.00
38	Rent and rates	24,600.00	14,350.00	12,300.00	6,560.00	4,320.00	62,730.00
39	Machine insurance	3,340.00	2,087.50	1,670.00	835.00	417.50	8,350.00
40	Depreciation	6,580.00	4,112.50	3,290.00	1,645.00	822.50	16,450.00
41	Production supervisor	13,791.89	3,940.54	6,567.57			24,300.00
42	Heat and light	3,450.98	2,013.07	1,725.49	320.26	690.20	8,800.00
43	*Subtotals*	56,562.87	28,703.61	29,053.06	11,360.26	8,450.20	
44	Absorption of costs of Dept M	2,392.05	6,936.95	2,631.26			
45	Absorption of costs of Dept R	4,647.61	1,521.04	2,281.55			
46	TOTALS	63,602.53	37,161.60	33,965.87			
49	**Absorption rate**						
50							
51		**Dept C**	**Dept F**	**Dept A**			
52		£	£	£			
53	Rate per labour hour	15.14	30.97	16.98			

The formulae are displayed in the illustaration below. As Column A contains text rather than formulae it has been excluded from this picture.

B (Dept C)	C (Dept F)	D (Dept A)	E (Dept H)	F (Dept R)	G (Total)
Dept C	Dept F	Dept A	Dept H	Dept R	
3000	1750	1500	800	600	
32000	20000	16000	8000	4000	
4.1	5.14	4.25	4	3.2	
4200	1200	2000			
Total					
£					
=SUM(B10:F10)*3.2					
£350					
16.450					
24300					
£300					
=SUM(B19:B23)					
Dept C	Dept F	Dept A	Dept H	Dept R	
4800	2200	3500	2000	1600	
0.2	0.58	0.22			
0.55	0.18	0.27			
Dept C	Dept F	Dept A	Dept H	Dept R	Total
=B24	=C24	=D24	=E24	=F24	
=B$19*B10/SUM($B10:$F10)	=B$19*C10/SUM($B10:$F10)	=B$19*D10/SUM($B10:$F10)	=B$19*E10/SUM($B10:$F10)	=B$19*F10/SUM($B10:$F10)	=IF(SUM(B37:F37)=SUM(B29:F29),SUM(B37:F37),"ERROR"
=B$20*B11/SUM($B11:$F11)	=B$20*C11/SUM($B11:$F11)	=B$20*D11/SUM($B11:$F11)	=B$20*E11/SUM($B11:$F11)	=B$20*F11/SUM($B11:$F11)	=IF(SUM(B38:F38)=B19,SUM(B38:F38),"ERROR")
=B$21*B11/SUM($B11:$F11)	=B$21*C11/SUM($B11:$F11)	=B$21*D11/SUM($B11:$F11)	=B$21*E11/SUM($B11:$F11)	=B$21*F11/SUM($B11:$F11)	=IF(SUM(B39:F39)=B20,SUM(B39:F39),"ERROR")
=B$22*B13/SUM($B13:$F13)	=B$22*C13/SUM($B13:$F13)	=B$22*D13/SUM($B13:$F13)			=IF(SUM(B40:F40)=B21,SUM(B40:F40),"ERROR")
=B$23*B10/SUM($B10:$F10)	=B$23*C10/SUM($B10:$F10)	=B$23*D10/SUM($B10:$F10)	=B$23*E10/SUM($B10:$F10)	=B$23*F10/SUM($B10:$F10)	=IF(SUM(B41:F41)=B22,SUM(B41:F41),"ERROR")
=SUM(B37:B42)	=SUM(C37:C42)	=SUM(D37:D42)	=SUM(E37:E42)	=SUM(F37:F42)	=IF(SUM(B42:F42)=B23,SUM(B42:F42),"ERROR")
=E43*B30	=E43*C30	=E43*D30			
=F43*B31	=F43*C31	=F43*D31			
=SUM(B43:B45)	=SUM(C43:C45)	=SUM(D43:D45)			

(g)   See solution to part (h)

(h)

Wild Thyme Ltd
Overhead apportionment
Budgeted figures
Year ending 31 December 20X7

Departmental statistics

	Dept C	Dept F	Dept A	Dept M	Dept R
Floor area (sq. m)	3,000	1,750	1,500	800	600
Plant value	£32,000	£20,000	£16,000	£8,000	£4,000
Hourly labour rate	£4.10	£5.14	£4.25	£4.00	£3.20
Direct labour hours	4,200	1,200	2,000	-	-

Departmental overheads

	Totals
	£
Rent and rates	62,730
Machine insurance	8,350
Depreciation	16,450
Production supervisor	24,300
Heat and light	8,800
	120,630

Allocated overheads

	Dept C	Dept F	Dept A	Dept M	Dept R
Specific to department	£4,800	£2,200	£3,500	£2,000	£1,600
Dept M	20%	58%	22%		
Dept R	55%	18%	27%		

Apportionment calculation

	Dept C	Dept F	Dept A	Dept M	Dept R	Total
Costs specific to department	4,800.00	2,200.00	3,500.00	2,000.00	1,600.00	14,100.00
Rent and rates	24,600.00	14,350.00	12,300.00	6,560.00	4,920.00	62,730.00
Machine insurance	3,340.00	2,087.50	1,670.00	835.00	417.50	8,350.00
Depreciation	6,580.00	4,112.50	3,290.00	1,645.00	822.50	16,450.00
Production supervisor	13,791.89	3,940.54	6,567.57	-	-	24,300.00
Heat and light	3,450.98	2,013.07	1,725.49	920.26	690.20	8,800.00
Subtotals	56,562.87	28,703.61	29,053.06	11,960.26	8,450.20	
Absorption of costs of Dept M	2,392.05	6,936.95	2,631.26			
Absorption of costs of Dept R	4,647.61	1,521.04	2,281.55			
TOTALS	63,602.53	37,161.60	33,965.87			

Absorption rate

	Dept C	Dept F	Dept A
	£	£	£
Rate per labour hour	15.14	30.97	16.98

(i) No written solution given.

(j) Only two cells need to be changed.

Wild Thyme Ltd
Overhead apportionment
Budgeted figures
Year ending 31 December 20X7

Departmental statistics

	Dept C	Dept F	Dept A	Dept M	Dept R
Floor area (sq. m)	3,000	1,750	1,500	800	600
Plant value	£32,000	£20,000	£16,000	£8,000	£4,000
Hourly labour rate	£4.10	£5.14	£4.25	£4.00	£3.20
Direct labour hours	4,200	1,200	2,000	-	-

Departmental overheads

	Totals £
Rent and rates	62,730
Machine insurance	8,350
Depreciation	16,450
Production supervisor	25,200
Heat and light	3,500
	122,230

Allocated overheads

	Dept C	Dept F	Dept A	Dept M	Dept R
Specific to department	£4,800	£2,200	£3,500	£2,000	£1,600
Dept M	20%	58%	22%		
Dept R	55%	18%	27%		

Apportionment calculation

	Dept C	Dept F	Dept A	Dept M	Dept R	Total
Costs specific to department	4,800.00	2,200.00	3,500.00	2,000.00	1,600.00	14,100.00
Rent and rates	24,600.00	14,350.00	12,300.00	6,560.00	4,320.00	62,730.00
Machine insurance	3,340.00	2,087.50	1,670.00	835.00	417.50	8,350.00
Depreciation	6,580.00	4,112.50	3,290.00	1,645.00	822.50	16,450.00
Production supervisor	14,302.70	4,086.43	6,810.81	-	-	25,200.00
Heat and light	3,725.49	2,173.20	1,862.75	993.46	745.10	3,500.00
Subtotals	57,348.19	29,009.63	29,433.56	12,033.46	8,505.10	
Absorption of costs of Dept M	2,406.69	6,979.41	2,647.36			
Absorption of costs of Dept R	4,677.80	1,530.92	2,296.38			
TOTALS	64,432.69	37,520.02	34,377.29			

Absorption rate

	Dept C £	Dept F £	Dept A £
Rate per labour hour	15.34	31.27	17.19

(k) No written solution given.

SOLUTION TO PRACTICE DEVOLVED ASSESSMENT 3: ISLAND QUAY

Parts of the solution are available in the BPP file **DA3_S**. The password to open this is:

LARGER

(a)   Refer solution to part (e). Given that it is quite difficult to follow what is required or how the information will fit together it is perhaps best to enter it as the instructions are given (at least initially).

(b)   Refer solution to part (e).

(c)   No written solution given.

(d)   This suggests that the disk on which the file is stored may be corrupted. The first thing to do is to stop processing. Do not attempt to save any other files onto the disk. There may be a simple solution, for example, if you are working on a network, another user may be using your file, but unless you now exactly what you are doing and/or error messages are more informative than this one, you should refer the problem to some-one who has technical expertise.

(e)   Well done if your answer looks anything like the following. This is deliberately a very difficult devolved assessment.

	A	B	C	D	E	F	G
1	**Island Quay plc**						
2	**Customer Services Department**						
3	**Performance report**		Year 1	Year 2	Year 3	Year 4	
4							
5	*Inflation*						
6	General price deflator	(1)	1.00	1.04	1.08	1.13	1.19
7							
8	*Capital*						
9			£	£	£	£	
10	Value of capital at start of year	(2)	180,000.00	149,760.00	116,640.00	81,360.00	42,840.00
11	Annual capital charge	(3)	47,541.60	46,764.00	45,810.00	45,027.00	
12	Physical capital consumed	(4)	47,541.60	44,965.38	42,416.67	39,846.90	
13							
14	*Running costs*						
15	Hours worked	(5)	30,000.00	30,000.00	30,000.00	30,000.00	
16			£	£	£	£	
17	Labour costs	(6)	205,000.00	200,000.00	204,000.00	208,080.00	
18	Average wacte rate	(7)	6.83	6.67	6.80	6.94	
19	Other running costs	(8)	62,000.00	64,000.00	66,000.00	64,000.00	
20	Physical other running costs	(9)	62,000.00	61,538.46	61,111.11	56,637.17	
21							
22	*Totals*						
23			£	£	£	£	
24	Total annual cost	(10)	314,541.60	310,764.00	315,810.00	317,107.00	
25	Total physical running costs	(11)	267,000.00	266,538.46	266,111.11	261,637.17	
26	Total physical resources consumed	(12)	314,541.60	311,503.85	308,527.78	301,484.07	
27							
28	*Outputs*						
29			No	No	No	No	
30	Warranties issued (W)	(13)	6,400.00	6,800.00	6,800.00	7,000.00	
31	Repairs performed (R)	(14)	620.00	700.00	640.00	660.00	
32							
33	*Unit costs*						
34			£	£	£	£	
35	Total costs: warranties issued	(15)	15,727.08	15,538.20	15,790.50	15,855.35	
36	Unit cost of issuing warranties	(16)	2.46	2.29	2.32	2.27	
37	Real unit cost of issuing warranties	(17)	2.46	2.20	2.15	2.00	
38	Total costs: repairs performed	(18)	188,724.96	186,458.40	189,486.00	190,264.20	
39	Unit cost of repairs performed	(19)	250.00	300.02	323.72	321.42	
40	Real unit cost of repairs performed	(20)	250.00	288.48	299.75	284.44	
41							
42	*Productivity*						
43			£	£	£	£	
44	Physical output of W & R	(21)	170,727.08	191,710.02	176,710.02	182,201.49	
45	Physical running costs: W & R	(22)	173,550.00	173,250.00	172,972.22	170,064.16	
46							
47	Productivity of running costs: W & R	(23)	0.984	1.107	1.022	1.071	
48	Year on year increase in (23)	(24)		12.50%	-7.68%	4.79%	
49			£	£	£	£	
50	Total physical resources consumed: W & R	(25)	204,452.04	202,477.50	200,543.06	195,964.65	
51							
52	Productivity of all resources: W & R	(26)	0.840	0.950	0.880	0.930	
53	Year on year increase in (26)	(27)		13.10%	-7.37%	5.68%	
54							
55	**Data table**						
56	Cost of capital		0.07				
57							

	A	B	C	D	E	F	G
3	**Performance report**		Year 1	Year 2	Year 3	Year 4	
4							
5	*Inflation*						
6	General price deflator	1	1	1.04	1.08	1.13	1.19
7							
8	*Capital*						
9			£	£	£	£	£
10	Value of capital at start	2	180000	=C$10*0.8*D6	=C$10*0.6*E6	=C$10*0.4*F6	=C$10*0.2*G6
11	Annual capital charge	3	=C10*(1/5)+($C$56*(C10+D10)/2	=D10*(1/4)+($C$56*(D10+E10)/2	=E10*(1/3)+($C$56*(E10+F10)/2	=F10*(1/2)+($C$56*(F10+G10)/2	
12	Physical capital consum	4	=C11/C6	=D11/D6	=E11/E6	=F11/F6	
13							
14	*Running costs*						
15	Hours worked	5	300000				
16			£	£	£	£	
17	Labour costs	6	205000	200000	=D17*1.02	=E17*1.02	
18	Average waste rate	7	=C17/C15	=D17/D15	=E17/E15	=F17/F15	
19	Other running costs	8	62000	64000	66000	64000	
20	Physical other running c	9	=C19/C6	=D19/D6	=E19/E6	=F19/F6	
21							
22	*Totals*						
23			£	£	£	£	
24	Total annual cost	10	=C11+C17+C19	=D11+D17+D19	=E11+E17+E19	=F11+F17+F19	
25	Total physical running c	11	=C20+(C15*$C$18)	=D20+(D15*$C$18)	=E20+(E15*$C$18)	=F20+(F15*$C$18)	
26	Total physical resource	12	=C12+C25	=D12+D25	=E12+E25	=F12+F25	
27							
28	*Outputs*						
29			No	No	No	No	
30	Warranties issued ('w')	13	6400	6800	6800	7000	
31	Repairs performed (R)	14	620	700	640	660	
32							
33	*Unit costs*						
34			£	£	£	£	
35	Total costs: warranties	15	=C24*0.05	=D24*0.05	=E24*0.05	=F24*0.05	
36	Unit cost of issuing war	16	=C35/C30	=D35/D30	=E35/E30	=F35/F30	
37	Real unit cost of issuing	17	=C36/C6	=D36/D6	=E36/E6	=F36/F6	
38	Total costs: repairs per	18	=C24*0.6	=D24*0.6	=E24*0.6	=F24*0.6	
39	Unit cost of repairs per	19	250	=C38*1.07*(D6/C6)/D31	=D38*1.07*(E6/D6)/E31	=E38*1.07*(F6/E6)/F31	
40	Real unit cost of repair:	20	=C39/C6	=D39/D6	=E39/E6	=F39/F6	
41							
42	*Productivity*						
43			£	£	£	£	
44	Physical output of W &	21	=C30*$C$36+C31*$C$39	=D30*$C$36+D31*$C$39	=E30*$C$36+E31*$C$39	=F30*$C$36+F31*$C$39	
45	Physical running costs:	22	=C25*0.65	=D25*0.65	=E25*0.65	=F25*0.65	
46							
47	Productivity of running	23	=ROUND(C44/C45,3)	=ROUND(D44/D45,3)	=ROUND(E44/E45,3)	=ROUND(F44/F45,3)	
48	Year on year increase in	24		=D47/C47-1	=E47/D47-1	=F47/E47-1	
49			£	£	£	£	
50	Total physical resource	25	=C26*0.65	=D26*0.65	=E26*0.65	=F26*0.65	
51							
52	Productivity of all resou	26	=ROUND(C44/C50,2)	=ROUND(D44/D50,2)	=ROUND(E44/E50,2)	=ROUND(F44/F50,2)	
53	Year on year increase in	27		=D52/C52-1	=E52/D52-1	=F52/E52-1	

SOLUTION TO PRACTICE DEVOLVED ASSESSMENT 4: YORK TOWN

Parts of the solution are available in the BPP file **DA4_S.** The password to open this is:

anfield

(a)   No written solution.

(b)   **Finding differences in the total cost column**

Columns G and H are used to re-calculate the total cost (this seems to be OK in column F but we can use formulae to cross-check the 2,000 rows of the worksheet). Column G contains *My Total* to recalculate total cost and column H shows the difference (if any) between the two columns.

	A	B	C	D	E	F	G	H
	Product Ref	Last Move Date	Product Name	Quantity	Unit Cost	Total Cost	My Total	Difference
2	100080	11-May-2000	PAPER FAX 164 FT 6 ROLLS SONGASING	31	42.23	1,309.13	1309.13	0.00
3	100165	08-Jun-2000	CD PLAYER PORT achiawa	3	38.80	116.40		
4	100186	08-Apr-2000	HEADPHONES STEREO achiawa WIRELESS	64	3.42	218.88		
5	100319	20-May-2000	VCR VHS 4HD NCC STEREO HIFI	22	7.99	175.78		
6	100536	30-May-2000	CD PLAYER SINGLE DISC achiawa	12	393.75	4,725.00		
7	100639	17-May-2000	VCR CABLE CONNECTORS BISCRENN	25	42.23	1,055.75		

The formulas used are:

Cell G2	Cell G3
=D2*E2	=F2-G2

These formulas can be copied down from rows G and H to obtain results for the other product lines.

The two total columns and the difference column can now be cast. The totals are shown below.

1986	998665	23-May-2000	WALKMAN AM/FM ST CASSETTE achiawa	19	78.75	1,496.25	1496.25	0.00
1987	998719	10-Jun-2000	COMPUTER PERFORMA 575 5MB RAM	1	550.99	550.99	550.99	0.00
1988	998809	10-Jun-2000	COMPUTER PentiumSX33MZ 4MB 210MB HD	1	625.00	625.00	625	0.00
1989	998889	18-Mar-2000	VCR VHS HIFI achiawa STEREO VCRPLUS	85	9.13	776.05	776.05	0.00
1990	998955	24-Feb-2000	VCR ADAPTOR LENMAR	107	5.71	610.97	610.97	0.00
1991	998970	01-Apr-2000	CD PLAYER PORT achiawa	71	26.25	1,863.75	1863.75	0.00
1992	999049	21-May-2000	PAPER FAX 164FT 2 ROLLS UNIFAX	21	41.09	862.89	862.89	0.00
1993	999066	05-Jun-2000	VCR VHS 12PNP ON SCREEN MTS NCC	6	33.10	198.60	198.6	0.00
1994	999302	10-Jun-2000	AV STEREO RECEIVER KKL 120WATTS	1	142.66	142.66	142.66	0.00
1995	999757	09-Jun-2000	CD PLAYER MULTI DISC VOYAGER	2	225.88	451.76	451.76	0.00
1996	999815	11-May-2000	TV 31" NCC STEREO MONITOR	31	13.70	424.70	424.7	0.00
1997								
1998			Totals			16,009,346.96	16,089,848.45	-80,501.49

The formulas used are:

Cell F1998	Cell G1998	Cell H1998
=SUM(F2:F1996)	= SUM(G2:G1996)	= SUM(G2:G1996)

The total difference found is £80,501.49.

Finding reasons for the difference between two total cost columns

Sorting the data on the difference column in ascending order shows that there is a difference in the calculation for all items with a unit quantity of 100.

	A	B	C	D	E	F	G	H
1	Product Ref	Last Move Date	Product Name	Quantity	Unit Cost	Total Cost	My Total	Difference
2	891121	03-Mar-2000	VCP VHS PLAYER HIFI SILVERBADGE	100	311.14	0.32	31114	-31,113.68
3	908841	03-Mar-2000	PORT TV 5" achiawa COLOR CRT WHITE	100	210.97	0.47	21097	-21,096.53
4	302654	03-Mar-2000	HARD DRIVE 342MB INTERNAL	100	101.58	0.98	10158	-10,157.02
5	473598	03-Mar-2000	MODEM INTERNAL 14.4 FAX PRODIGY	100	92.45	1.08	9245	-9,243.92
6	994861	03-Mar-2000	PAPER FAX 6ROLLS 328FT UNIFAX	100	71.90	1.39	7190	-7,188.61
7	414876	03-Mar-2000	VCR VHS 4HD PULTSAR STEREO HIFI	100	13.70	7.30	1370	-1,362.70
8	482782	03-Mar-2000	TV BASE achiawa	100	3.42	29.24	342	-312.76
9	706970	03-Mar-2000	VCR VHS 4HD NCC HIFI	100	1.14	87.72	114	-26.28
10	100080	11-May-2000	PAPER FAX 164 FT 6 ROLLS SONGASING	31	42.23	1,309.13	1309.13	0.00

Compare the formulae in F2 and G2. The stock controller has used a formula which divided when it should have multiplied. The total cost formulae should be amended to correct this error.

Also note that the last move date is the same for all of these items. This may be a further error and should be queried with stores staff.

Reviewing unit cost and quantity columns

The easiest method of reviewing these columns is to sort them and then look for unusual items (such as negative balances) at the top or bottom of the lists.

Negative stock balances

Sorting the data on the quantity field shows that some stock balances have been entered as negative items. This has the effect of undervaluing stock. Amending the quantities to show positive values provides an increase in the stock valuation from **16,090,236.45**to **16,207,437.85**, an increase of **117,201.40**. The stock lines affected are shown below.

	A	B	C	D	E	F	G
1	Product Ref	Last Move Date	Product Name	Quantity	Unit Cost	Total Cost	My Total
2	177235	01-Jun-2000	CD PLAYER US DIAMOND CAR KIT	-10	19.40	-194.00	-194.00
3	219403	01-Jun-2000	SOFTWARE MICROSOFT SIMULATOR 6.0	-10	73.04	-730.40	-730.40
4	254098	01-Jun-2000	TV 32" TOSHIBA STEREO MTR PIP-2	-10	696.19	-6,961.90	-6961.90
5	271868	01-Jun-2000	PORT TV CASIO 1.6" COLOR W/	-10	402.88	-4,028.80	-4028.80
6	322408	01-Jun-2000	MEMORY STANDARD SIMMS USE FOR	-10	22.83	-228.30	-228.30
7	329153	01-Jun-2000	FACSIMILE MACHINE MULTI-ELEC	-10	342.39	-3,423.90	-3423.90
8	357392	01-Jun-2000	CLOCK RADIO AM/FM DIGITAL achiawa	-10	2.28	-22.80	-22.80
9	423102	01-Jun-2000	TV 20" ZENITH ST MTR RMT "CC"	-10	249.99	-2,499.90	-2499.90
10	459806	01-Jun-2000	COMPUTER FAX SWITCH COMMAND	-10	20.54	-205.40	-205.40
11	463902	01-Jun-2000	VIDEO ADAPTER SPLITTER-COMBINER	-10	83.31	-833.10	-833.10
12	491974	01-Jun-2000	NOTEBOOK PentiumDX2/50SL SHARP	-10	1,505.00	-15,050.00	-15050.00
13	564236	01-Jun-2000	DISKS DOUBLESIDED FUJI 5 1/4" 10	-10	2.25	-22.50	-22.50
14	630399	01-Jun-2000	BATTERY CR123	-10	7.99	-79.90	-79.90
15	648647	01-Jun-2000	FAX MODEM VOICE MAIL	-10	57.07	-570.70	-570.70
16	662230	01-Jun-2000	LASER PRINTER 10 PPM 1MB RAM	-10	270.49	-2,704.90	-2704.90
17	678879	01-Jun-2000	VCR TAPE HI8 MP 60MIN TIMES	-10	6.65	-66.50	-66.50
18	744414	01-Jun-2000	CD PLAYER MULTI DISC achiawa	-10	505.87	-5,058.70	-5058.70
19	761605	01-Jun-2000	CD PLAYER SINGLE PLAY VOYAGER	-10	52.50	-525.00	-525.00
20	765870	01-Jun-2000	BATTERY 9V 2 PACK ENERGIZER	-10	34.24	-342.40	-342.40
21	772929	01-Jun-2000	LASER PRINTER 1MB PCL5 ADVANCED	-10	207.72	-2,077.20	-2077.20
22	781793	01-Jun-2000	GAME CD STARBLADE TAGA	-10	36.99	-369.90	-369.90
23	878036	01-Jun-2000	VCR TAPE VHS TRL HIGH GRADE	-10	47.93	-479.30	-479.30
24	912330	01-Jun-2000	VCR TAPE 8MM achiawa	-10	2.25	-22.50	-22.50
25	924635	01-Jun-2000	COMPUTER NOTEBOOK PentiumDX33 4MB	-10	1,199.99	-11,999.90	-11999.90
26	983602	01-Jun-2000	PRINTER BUBBLEJET Smithie	-10	23.97	-239.70	-239.70
27	991208	01-Jun-2000	VCR VHS 4HD achiawa VCR PLUS+	-10	5.71	-57.10	-57.10

Negative Unit costs

Sorting the data on the Unit Cost field shows that some stock balances have been entered into the database with negative values. This also has the effect of undervaluing stock. Amending the values to positive amounts provides an increase in the stock valuation from **16,207,437.85** to **16,434,952.39**, an increase of **– 227,514.54**. The stock lines affected are shown in the following illustration.

	A	B	C	D	E	F	G
1	Product Ref	Last Move Date	Product Name	Quantity	Unit Cost	Total Cost	My Total
2	455793	09-May-2000	TV 31" MITSUBISHI ST MTR "CC"	33	-336.68	-11,110.44	-11110.44
3	839424	26-Dec-1999	TV 27" ZENITH STEREO MONITOR RMT	167	-336.68	-56,225.56	-56225.56
4	500806	10-Jun-2000	BATTERY CHGR/SAVER FOR PC305	1	-335.54	-335.54	-335.54
5	822934	03-Jun-2000	TV 20" ZENITH REMOTE	8	-335.54	-2,684.32	-2684.32
6	382629	14-Apr-2000	TV 27" ZENITH CONSOLE ST RMT PIP	58	-335.54	-19,461.32	-19461.32
7	934070	08-Jun-2000	TV 20" HITACHI STEREO REMOTE BLK	3	-333.26	-999.78	-999.78
8	580631	03-Jun-2000	WALKMAN STEREO CASSETTE MULTI-ELEC	8	-332.12	-2,656.96	-2656.96
9	573279	10-Jun-2000	BATTERY C 4 PACK ENERGIZER	1	-220.27	-220.27	-220.27
10	719585	08-Jun-2000	BATT ELIM/CHARGER FOR	3	-220.27	-660.81	-660.81
11	156881	06-Jun-2000	CD PLAYER SINGLE PLAY USDIAMOND	5	-220.27	-1,101.35	-1101.35
12	587232	09-Jun-2000	RAM CARD MACINTOSH LINK II SHARP	2	-110.71	-221.42	-221.42
13	553506	29-May-2000	TV 30" TOSHIBA ST MTR PIP "CC"	13	-110.71	-1,439.23	-1439.23
14	556894	14-Apr-2000	TV 27" BISCRENN ST MTR RMT	58	-110.71	-6,421.18	-6421.18
15	528300	19-Mar-2000	TV RACK GUSDORF	84	-110.71	-9,299.64	-9299.64
16	828471	31-May-2000	HEADPHONE STEREO achiawa	11	-76.55	-842.05	-842.05
17	401994	09-Jun-2000	DISKETTE 3.5" IBM FORMATED	2	-25.00	-50.00	-50.00
18	829433	10-Jun-2000	PORT TV COLOR WATCHMAN CASIO	1	-22.83	-22.83	-22.83
19	565563	10-Jun-2000	FAX MACHINE USDIAMOND	1	-4.57	-4.57	-4.57

The revised stock valuation is on the *Stock Valuation* sheet in the workbook.

Stock provision

Stock provision is calculated firstly by finding the age of the individual stock items and then by applying a percentage provision to each category of stock.

Stock ageing

The number of days since each stock line last moved is calculated by taking the date value for the year-end away from the last moved date.

	A	B	C	D	E	F	G	H
1	Product Ref	Last Move Date	Product Name	Quantity	Unit Cost	Total Cost	Year-end	Stock Age
2	100080	11-May-2000	PAPER FAX 164 FT 6 ROLLS SONGASING	31	42.23	1,309.13	30-Jun-2000	49

Cell G2 is *Date* formatted using the same format as B2. This format can be copied from cell B2 or applied from the *Format | Cells* dialog box.

Cell H2 contains the formula =DAYS360(B2,G2) which gives the difference between the two dates.

Stock valuation based on ageing

The stock ageing can now be determined by comparing the **Stock Age** number with the required ageing analysis.

	D	E	F	G	H	I	J	K	L
1	Quantity	Unit Cost	Total Cost	Year-end	Stock Ag	Age < 90	Age 91 < 1{	Age 181 < 3{	Age > 360
2	31	42.23	1,309.13	30-Jun-2000	49	1309.13	0	0	0
3	3	38.80	116.40	30-Jun-2000	22	116.4	0	0	0
4	64	3.42	218.88	30-Jun-2000	82	218.88	0	0	0
5	22	7.99	175.78	30-Jun-2000	40	175.78	0	0	0
6	12	393.75	4,725.00	30-Jun-2000	30	4725	0	0	0
7	25	42.23	1,055.75	30-Jun-2000	43	1055.75	0	0	0
8	12	70.76	849.12	30-Jun-2000	30	849.12	0	0	0
9	95	1.14	108.30	30-Jun-2000	112	0	108.3	0	0
10	83	216.85	17,998.55	30-Jun-2000	100	0	17998.55	0	0
11	167	825.25	137,816.75	30-Jun-2000	184	0	0	137816.75	0
12	2	4.57	9.14	30-Jun-2000	21	9.14	0	0	0
13	3	20.54	61.62	30-Jun-2000	22	61.62	0	0	0

The formulas for each of the cells are:

I2	J2
=IF(H2<=90,F2,0)	=IF(H2>90,IF(H2<=180,F2,0),0)

K2	L2
=IF(H2>180,IF(H2<=360,F2,0),0)	=IF(H2>360,F2,0)

The totals for the ageing analysis are:

	D	E	F	G	H	I	J	K	L
1990	107	5.71	610.97	30-Jun-2000	126	0	610.97	0	0
1991	71	26.25	1,863.75	30-Jun-2000	89	1863.75	0	0	0
1992	21	41.09	862.89	30-Jun-2000	39	862.89	0	0	0
1993	6	33.10	198.60	30-Jun-2000	25	198.6	0	0	0
1994	1	142.66	142.66	30-Jun-2000	20	142.66	0	0	0
1995	2	225.88	451.76	30-Jun-2000	21	451.76	0	0	0
1996	31	13.70	424.70	30-Jun-2000	49	424.7	0	0	0
1997									
1998			16,434,952.39			4,744,819.69	3,920,399.46	3,257,695.01	4,512,038.23

Comparing the total to the total cost field can check the accuracy of the analysis (that is to ensure that all lines are included in the total).

(c)   Refer to DA4_S.xls in the BPP data files

(d)   **Stock provision**

The stock provision can now be calculated based on the ageing analysis of stock. The total provision required is £5,992,976.04. The break down between the different age groups is shown below:

	F	G	H	I	J	K	L	M
1990	610.97	30-Jun-2000	126	0	610.97	0	0	
1991	1,863.75	30-Jun-2000	89	1863.75	0	0	0	
1992	862.89	30-Jun-2000	39	862.89	0	0	0	
1993	198.60	30-Jun-2000	25	198.6	0	0	0	
1994	142.66	30-Jun-2000	20	142.66	0	0	0	
1995	451.76	30-Jun-2000	21	451.76	0	0	0	
1996	424.70	30-Jun-2000	49	424.7	0	0	0	
1997								Total
1998	16,434,952.39			4,744,819.69	3,920,399.46	3,257,695.01	4,512,038.23	16,434,952.39
1999								
2000		Provision %			25%	50%	75%	
2001								
2002		Provision required			980,099.87	1,628,847.51	3,384,028.67	5,992,976.04

The ageing analysis is shown on the *Ageing* worksheet.

Chart to show ageing analysis

A chart showing the value of each stock and the provision required is shown below.

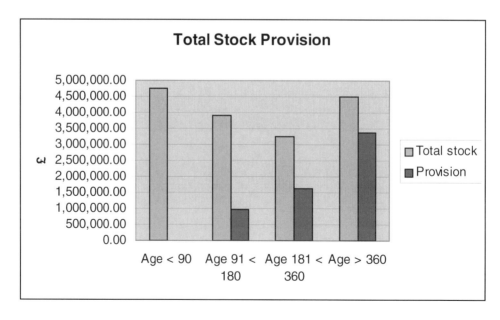

The data to produce this chart is shown starting a cell H2006 on the *Ageing* worksheet. The data is placed in one block to make production of the chart easier.

(e) **Further analysis on computer stock**

Information on computers only is copied to a separate sheet after sort the main data on the product description column. All computer items appear to start with the word computer.

Computer stock provision

The ageing provision is calculated in the same method as for the main data; the results are shown below.

	D	E	F	G	H	I	J	K	L
86	6	1,099.99	6,599.94	30-Jun-2000	25	6,599.94	0.00	0.00	0.00
87	1	1,500.00	1,500.00	30-Jun-2000	20	1,500.00	0.00	0.00	0.00
88	1	999.99	999.99	30-Jun-2000	20	999.99	0.00	0.00	0.00
89	4	1,099.95	4,399.80	30-Jun-2000	23	4,399.80	0.00	0.00	0.00
90	291	1,199.99	349,197.09	30-Jun-2000	306	0.00	0.00	349,197.09	0.00
91	474	1,199.99	568,795.26	30-Jun-2000	487	0.00	0.00	0.00	568,795.26
92	18	1,299.99	23,399.82	30-Jun-2000	36	23,399.82	0.00	0.00	0.00
93									
94						598,278.48	350,628.41	1,555,249.24	1,107,445.26
95									
96				Provision %			25%	50%	75%
97									
98				Provision required			87,657.10	777,624.62	830,583.95

Chart showing computer stock ageing

Again, this is calculated in the same way as for the chart showing the main stock analysis.

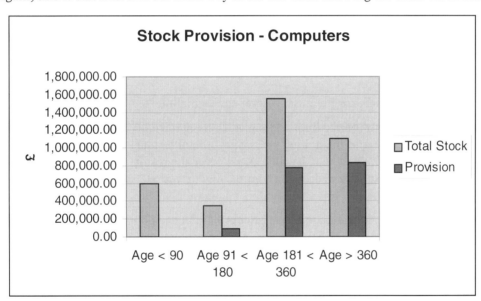

Reasons for inadequate computer stock ageing.

The computer ageing may be inadequate for two main reasons. Firstly, some of the computer lines have not moved for over 90 days. Given that computer technology moves very quickly, it is likely to be difficult to sell these computers because they are already becoming obsolete. Additional provision will therefore be required.

Secondly, some of the computers appear to be old, even though units have been sold within the last 90 days. An analysis of the product name field shows some computers are still in stock based on very old processor types (such as 286!). Although the valuation is not significant for these items, full provision can now be made because it is unlikely that these older systems will be sold.

Revised stock provision:

The revised stock provision makes full provision against any 286 computer in column M of the worksheet.

	E	F	G	H	I	J	K	L	M	N
83	85.60	85.60	30-Jun-00	20	85.60	0.00	0.00	0.00		
84	5.71	5.71	30-Jun-00	20	5.71	0.00	0.00	0.00		
85	1,099.99	1,099.99	30-Jun-00	20	1,099.99	0.00	0.00	0.00		
86	999.95	999.95	30-Jun-00	20	999.95	0.00	0.00	0.00		
87	1,399.95	1,399.95	30-Jun-00	20	1,399.95	0.00	0.00	0.00		
88	999.00	999.00	30-Jun-00	20	999.00	0.00	0.00	0.00		
89	550.99	550.99	30-Jun-00	20	550.99	0.00	0.00	0.00		
90	550.99	550.99	30-Jun-00	20	550.99	0.00	0.00	0.00		
91	1,500.00	1,500.00	30-Jun-00	20	1,500.00	0.00	0.00	0.00		
92	999.99	999.99	30-Jun-00	20	999.99	0.00	0.00	0.00		
93										**Total**
94					598,278.48	350,628.41	1,555,249.24	1,107,445.26	46,257.25	3,657,858.64
95										
96			Provision %			25%	100%	100%	100%	
97										
98			Provision required			87,657.10	1,555,249.24	1,107,445.26	46,257.25	2,796,608.85

The solution can be found on the worksheet *Amended Computer Stock.*

(f) **REPORT**

To: Financial Accountant
From   Assistant Accountant
Date   July 2000
Subject: Review of Stock Valuation report

This document summarises my findings regarding the Stock Valuation report.

Findings

1   Errors were found in the calculation of the total stock value:

- Negative quantities and negative values for individual stock lines were found

- In some instances total cost was derived by dividing quantity by price, rather than multipying.

2   Other discrepencies or potential discrepencies include:

- On the computer ageing worksheet, there appears to be a correlation between the age of stock and the quantity of stock – the older the stock then the more units are in stock. The data may be correct, however the results do appear to be unusual and should be invetigated. If the figures are correct, we should be concerned over the high level of obsolete stock held.

- The report does not appear to be complete. A memo from the controller noted that there would be 2002 stock items, however the report only includes 1995 items.

3   A bar chart showing the aged value of stock lines is shown below.

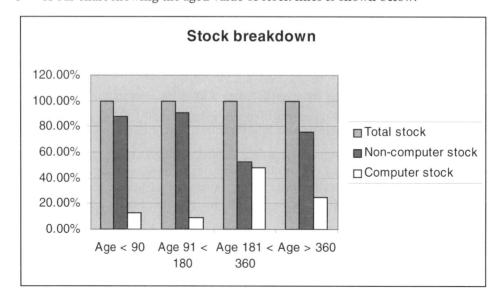

4   The stock report can be improved as outlined below.

- Implementing checks within the report and in the input process to the stock system which provided the information. Basic input validation routines will help to identify negative prices and stock quantities.

- Checking the data for reasonableness before it is sent to other departments. Reviewing the stock lines or performing the sort routines on the quantity and price columns would highlight the errors in the report.

- Provision of more pricing information to ensure that old stock is not overvalued.

- Checking for duplicate items. Some duplicate stock codes were noted.

5   The 10 highest value stock lines are:

Product Ref	Last Move Date	Product Name	Quantity	Unit Cost	Total Cost
812049	03-Aug-1994	TV 35" MITSUBISHI STEREO MTR PIP	1408	887.99	1,250,289.92
933666	08-Feb-1998	TV 35" MITSUBISHI STEREO MONITOR	853	887.99	757,455.47
301629	23-Feb-1999	COMPUTER SYSTEM PentiumSX25 4MB 129	474	1,199.99	568,795.26
397244	22-Nov-1998	COMPUTER PentiumDX2 66MZ 4MB RAM	567	950.00	538,650.00
847633	17-Mar-1999	TV 35" MITSUBISHI STEREO MTR	451	887.99	400,483.49
682738	06-Feb-1999	TV 32" achiawa PIP-2 MTR RMT "CC"	491	799.99	392,795.09
948435	05-Jul-1999	COMPUTER PentiumDX2 HORDING CD ROM	341	1,050.00	358,050.00
485805	24-Aug-1999	COMPUTER SYSTEM PentiumDX250 IBM	291	1,199.99	349,197.09
542781	20-Jul-1999	COMPUTER PentiumDX2 66MZ 8MB RAM	326	960.00	312,960.00
732735	06-Aug-1999	COMPUTER PentiumDX2 50MZ 4MB RAM 253	309	899.95	278,084.55
Total					5,206,760.87

These lines represent about 31% of the total stock value.

Please advise if you would like further action or investigation of this matter.

Accounting Technician

BPP
PUBLISHING

Solutions to Trial Run Devolved Assessments

SOLUTION TO TRIAL RUN DEVOLVED ASSESSMENT 5: MARVELS LTD

For a suggested answer look at the BPP file **DA5_S**. The password to open this spreadsheet is given at the end of this solution.

Task 1

The columns need resizing to accommodate all the information they hold. They should be given headings where they lack them, and these should be emphasised by formatting. It is usual to right align money amounts (the 30, 60, 90 day and Total columns). Most of the text items look best if they are left aligned.

It is useful to bring the monetary columns over next to the Customer names, since it is most likely to be these figures that will change most often and need to be worked on. Hopefully you were careful not to overwrite any information if you did this.

You should also **not leave any blank columns**, because this can affect how data is **sorted**.

Here is an extract from our suggested answer, showing improvements of this kind.

	A	B	C	D	E	F	G	H
1	Name	0-30	31-60	61-90	Total	Address 1	Address 2	Address 3
2	Fads	267.56	246.97	62.62	577.15	Putney High Street		
3	B & Q DIY Supercentre	1630.51	1087.00	168.24	2885.75	Blythwood Industrial Estate	Argyle Road	
4	D I Y Woodstock	786.56	524.37	15.92	1326.85	111 A Neilston Road		
5	D T S	657.14	537.66	66.60	1261.40	Chester Road East	Queensferry	
6	Tuck & Norris Ltd	504.12	756.18	72.50	1332.80	622 Lordship Lane		
7	Cardiff Paint Supplies	484.30	641.98	117.27	1243.55	51-53 Carlisle Street	Splott	
8	Great Mills D I Y	519.30	688.37	12.08	1219.75	Beardmore Park	Martlesham Heath	
9	Do-it-yourself	257.30	257.29	68.51	583.10	82 Niddrie Road		
10	Homecare Electrics	591.82	504.14	76.19	1172.15	6 Arndale Square		
11	Do It Yourself Supplies	1123.01	1550.82	69.12	2742.95	84 Church Road	Redfield	
12	Mercury Stores Hdwre Shop	457.91	607.00	29.89	1094.80	43 Chalcot Road		
13	Newmans	757.89	889.70	54.11	1701.70	31 Cherry Tree Avenue		
14	Bob Leach D I Y & Timber Store	1302.10	1023.08	245.22	2570.40	101 Botley Road	North Baddesley	
15	S D I Y Bill Centre	967.73	929.78	18.39	1915.90	8 Undercliff Road West		
16	D I Y Supplies	992.19	1315.23	233.23	2540.65	17 St James Street		
17	Pretty Chic	217.74	300.68	5.18	523.60	Greenhole Place	Bridge of Don	
18	Manor Utilities Hire Contractors	372.25	357.66	19.79	749.70	41 Bridge Road	Woolston	
19	Fads The Decorating Specialists	360.94	261.37	8.39	630.70	Glasgow (Easterhouse)	Unit 10	Township Centre
20	Murray Timber Supplies Timber & D I Y	61.91	44.83	0.36	107.10	3 The Mans	Mill Lane	
21	Scotts Hardware D I Y Shop	183.39	233.41	29.45	446.25	4 Ellenbrook Green		
22	Exmouth Handyman	594.29	820.69	54.67	1469.65	15 Exeter Road		
23	G Fox & Sons	1202.58	1155.42	248.10	2606.10	139 Clouds Hill Road	St George	
24	Do-it-yourself Supplies	317.59	330.56	24.20	672.35	35/37 New Street		
25	Great Mills D I Y Superstore	1367.89	950.56	204.35	2522.80	Rannoch Road	Birkenshaw Industrial Estate,	
26	Sullivans Home Improvement Centre	33.19	23.06	3.25	59.50	334 Gloucester Road	Horfield	
27	Fads	192.18	254.75	17.17	464.10	124 Rye Lane		
28	Homebase Ltd	1416.97	984.67	2.16	2403.80	Fox Den Road		
29	Rkp Hardware	1052.88	1095.85	5.17	2150.00	51 Englands Lane		
30	Walparite	1131.00	1499.23	59.17	2689.40	26 Bell Street		
31	R Hammersley	109.98	76.42	27.80	214.20	44 High Street		
32	A G Stanley Ltd	1052.69	1011.40	48.16	2112.25	224 Walworth Road		
33	Wasons Paint Paper & D I Y Centre	305.83	405.41	26.56	737.80	Office	43 Windsor Road	
34	Do It All Limited	760.59	730.76	19.95	1511.30	Wrexham	Holt Street	

The sheet should be given a name like **Marvels Ltd – Aged Debtors** (our answer, however, names sheets according to the Task that is being answered, for the sake of clarity.)

Task 2

For our coding system we have simply started numbering from 1 upwards. Numbers are shown as six figure numbers (000001) to allow for plenty of flexibility in the future (for instance up to 999,999 accounts!). There are of course many other possible coding systems and any sensible solution is acceptable here.

	A	B
1	**Code**	**Name**
2	000001	Fads
3	000002	B & Q DIY Supercentre
4	000003	D I Y Woodstock
5	000004	D T S
6	000005	Tuck & Norris Ltd
7	000006	Cardiff Paint Supplies
8	000007	Great Mills DIY Superstore
9	000008	Do-it-yourself
10	000009	Homecare Electrics
11	000010	Do It Yourself Supplies
12	000011	Mercury Stores Hdwre Shop
13	000012	Newmans
14	000013	Bob Leach D I Y & Timber Store
15	000014	S D I Y Bill Centre
16	000015	D I Y Supplies
17	000016	Pretty Chic
18	000017	Manor Utilities Hire Contractors
19	000018	Fads
20	000019	Murray Timber Supplies Timber & D I Y
21	000020	Scotts Hardware D I Y Shop
22	000021	Exmouth Handyman
23	000022	G Fox & Sons
24	000023	Do-it-yourself Supplies
25	000024	Great Mills DIY Superstore
26	000025	Sullivans Home Improvement Centre
27	000026	Fads
28	000027	Homebase Ltd
29	000028	Rkp Hardware
30	000029	Walparite
31	000030	R Hammersley
32	000031	A G Stanley Ltd
33	000032	Wasons Paint Paper & D I Y Centre
34	000033	Do It All Ltd
35	000034	Sullivans Home Improvement Centre
36	000035	D I Y Whitchurch
37	000036	Golders Green D I Y
38	000037	Timber & Tools
39	000038	Spectrum Home & Garden Centre
40	000039	Treasure Finder Ii

It is important that you put in your codes before you do any of the sorting of data that is useful for the remainder of this Task. There may be some significance in the order in which customers are entered. We do not know whether there is or not yet, so it is sensible to preserve the original order, at least for now.

We give all the B & Q stores the name 'B & Q DIY Supercentre', since this is the name that recurs most frequently.

'Do It All Ltd' is the most common form, so we have standardised these entries.

'Fads' appears simply as 'Fads' most often so this is the form we use throughout.

Other standards are 'Focus DIY Ltd' (no spaces), 'Great Mills DIY Superstore', 'Homebase Ltd' ('Sainsbury's Homebase' has also been changed to this), 'Homestyle', 'Texas Homecare Ltd', 'Wickes Building Supplies Ltd'.

The above were the only accounts that we meant you to edit so that they have the same names. There are, however, many names that you may have considered worth noting down for further investigation. Score marks if you made such a note, and no marks if you neglected this part of the task. There is no 'right' answer.

We made it easier to pick out possible similar names by sorting the data by name and then using a temporary formula in column O. We did this after **hiding** the intervening rows temporarily – as shown on the following illustration.

	A	B	O	P	Q	R	S
1	Code	Name					
2	000067	1st Stop D-i-y					
3	000188	A G Direct					
4	000031	A G Stanley Ltd					
5	000169	A S Gill					
6	000210	A S Golding	1				
7	000196	A T D I Y Layzell					
8	000198	Abbasi D I Y					
9	000389	Aber Valley D I Y					
10	000040	Ace Decore Colour & Design Centre					
11	000324	Ace Supply D I Y Ltd	1				
12	000239	Adaptions					
13	000251	Albert Dawson Ltd					
14	000290	Albrion Sales Ltd					
15	000334	Allen Bernard					
16	000407	Allwares					
17	000374	Arnold Laver Ltd					
18	000265	Art & Wood Supplies Do It Yourself					
19	000362	Artorder Ltd					
20	000382	Atlas D I Y Centre					
21	000325	Autopaint International					
22	000166	Avanti Window Systems					
23	000002	B & Q DIY Supercentre					
24	000041	B & Q DIY Supercentre	1				
25	000053	B & Q DIY Supercentre	1				
26	000061	B & Q DIY Supercentre	1				
27	000072	B & Q DIY Supercentre	1				

=IF(LEFT(B2,4)=LEFT(B1,4),1,"")

This extracts the first four characters in one cell (the first four at the LEFT) and compares them with the first four in the cell above. If the characters are identical, a 1 is shown in the equivalent cell in column F; if not nothing is shown.

Duplicates can be found using a similar technique. In this instance we sorted by telephone numbers and then searched for duplicates using =IF(L2=L1,1,"") and so on. You can sum the column first to see if there are any duplicates at all (it will sum to more than 0 if there are).

	A	B	G	L	O	P	Q	R
145	000372	D I Y Electrics	125 Exeter Road	01496 378500				
146	000320	Do-it-yourself Electrics	125 Exeter Road	01496 378500				
147	000326	B & Q DIY Supercentre	L verton Retail Park	01496 389451				
148	000192	S D I Y Clutton	45 Temple Street	01496 613095				
149	000196	A T D I Y Layzell	137 Temple Street	01496 614379				
150	000278	D I Y At Layzells D I Y Supplies	137 Temple Street	01496 614379	1			
151	000068	Nimmak Security & DIY	Sauchiehall Street	0151 4411914				
152	000008	Do-it-yourself	82 Niddrie Road	0151 5343699				
153	000279	Miller D I Y Supplies	90 Springburn Way	0151 6698443				
154	000173	B & Q DIY Supercentre	21 Legatston Road	0151 7313355				
155	000201	B & Q DIY Supercentre	Shawfield Industrial Estate	0151 7581956				
156	000165	Texas Homecare Ltd	222 Nether Auldhouse Road	0151 7593130				
157	000215	B & Q DIY Supercentre	Strathkelvin Retail Park	0151 8735667				

=IF(L146=L145,1,"")

MEMO

To: Sami Johnswell
From: Accounting Technician
Date: 3 November 2000

Subject: Duplicate customer accounts

As you know, this week I have been having a close examination of the customer records. One of the matters that has come to light is that there are a number of instances where we appear to have opened two accounts for a single customer.

Trial run devolved assessments

Code	Name	Address 1	Telephone	Balance
000320	Do-it-yourself Electrics	125 Exeter Road	01496 378500	737.80
000372	D I Y Electrics	125 Exeter Road	01496 378500	1,552.95
				2,290.75
000196	A T D I Y Layzell	107 Temple Street	01496 614379	1,951.60
000278	D I Y At Layzells D I Y Supplies	107 Temple Street	01496 614379	1,029.35
				2,980.95
000090	Milton's Timbers	232 The Broadway	0191 3030377	1,481.55
000350	Milton's Timbers	232 The Broadway	0191 3030377	12.30
				1,493.85
000180	B & Q DIY Supercentre	Larch Drive	0191 9969039	1,862.35
000378	B & Q DIY Supercentre	2 Larch Drive	0191 9969039	71.40
				1,933.75

I trust you will pursue this as you see fit, and advise me of the outcome of any discussions with customers.

In addition, the following customers have identical phone numbers, but different names or addresses. Perhaps we could look into these accounts too, to see if they are duplicates.

Code	Name	Address 1	Post Code	Telephone	Balance
000107	Homebase Ltd	Rookery Way	NW9 6SS	0191 3008600	1,999.20
000244	Texas Homecare Ltd	Colindale Capitol Park	NW9 0EQ	0191 3008600	285.60
					2,284.80
000087	Focus DIY Ltd	Benton Park Road	NE7 7LX	0191 3141744	327.25
000434	Focus DIY Ltd	Unit 1 Westmorland Way	NE1 1AA	0191 3141744	1,541.05
					1,868.30
000214	Maxwells (Sunderland) Ltd	Old Co-op Buildings	NE9 5PJ	0191 5985360	321.30
000225	Maxwells D.I.Y	35 Sheriff High Way	NE9 5PJ	0191 5985360	1,892.10
					2,213.40
000241	Homebase Ltd	Syon Lane	TW7 5BT	0191 9584798	2,600.15
000246	Homebase Ltd	Brentford Capital Interchange	TW8 1XX	0191 9584798	2,142.00
					4,742.15

Task 3

Tutorial note. To generate information for this Task you could either use a Pivot Table (as we do in our answer) or use your spreadsheet's sorting and filtering facilities.

Our Pivot Table was set up, very simply, as shown below, and then we did some further calculations on the same sheet, as reflected in our report.

There is not a great deal to say about the information, but try to make some comments based on common business sense.

Quite a lot of painstaking care is needed to identify the discrepancies.

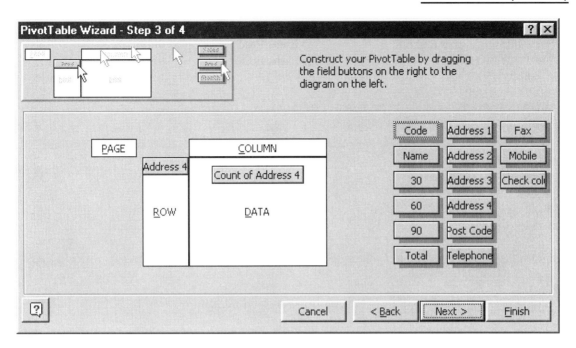

REPORT

To: Charles Davis
From: Accounting Technician
Date: 3 November 2000

Subject: Geographical sales patterns

Distribution is concentrated in the larger UK cities, especially London, but it is very widespread throughout the UK. A total of 105 different towns are represented amongst our 435 customer accounts. In Appendix One I list the top 30 towns, all of which have three customers or more.

The chief point to note here is that we have over five times as many customers in London than in the next best represented city, Bristol. Possibly our product is less well known outside the capital, or possibly there are problems in getting the product to distant locations.

The information suggests that marketing and distribution efforts in the future should concentrate on other major cities, notably Bristol, Leeds, Manchester, Glasgow, Birmingham, Newcastle and Southampton. Perhaps, in the not too distant future we could consider setting up other manufacturing bases outside London.

Note

The figures provided may be slightly misleading, because it is based on 'postal town' information entered into the customer records. If we look at postcodes we find that there are, for instance, 18 customers with a Birmingham post code, although not all of them have 'Birmingham' in their address.

However, I am not convinced that our customer address information is wholly accurate at present. I have compiled a list of matters to investigate.

Appendix One

Town	Customers	Cumulative	% (of 435)
London	117	117	
Bristol	23	140	
Leeds	18	158	
Manchester	18	176	
Glasgow	16	192	

BPP
PUBLISHING

Trial run devolved assessments

Town	Customers	Cumulative	% (of 435)
Birmingham	15	207	
Newcastle Upon Tyne	15	222	
Southampton	15	237	
Ipswich	11	248	
Cardiff	9	257	
Exeter	9	266	
Morecambe	8	274	
Chester	7	281	
Wrexham	7	288	
Aberdeen	5	293	
Eastleigh	5	298	
Canterbury	4	302	
Dover	4	306	
Dundee	4	310	
Enfield	4	314	
Exmouth	4	318	
Gateshead	4	322	
Newport	4	326	
Blackpool	3	329	
Deeside	3	332	
Fareham	3	335	
Harwich	3	338	
Lancaster	3	341	
Mold	3	344	
Paisley	3	347	

List of discrepancies in customer address information

Matters to investigate

Code	Name	Address 1	Address 2	Comment
000143	Redcroft	286 Chester Road		No postcode
000250	B & Q DIY Supercentre	Garthdee Road		No postcode
000304	Fairleys Ltd	36-38 Roker Avenue		No postcode

Errors to correct

Code	Name	Address 1	Address 2	Comment
000040	Ace Decore Colour & Design Centre	Unit 8 Clarence Street		Street name should be in Address 2 column
000131	Kemp Bros	High Street		Address 3 and 4, Telephone and fax are in the wrong columns,
000215	B & Q DIY Supercentre	Strathkelvin Retail Park		Fax number is nonsense (shown as 151, part of area code). Delete.
000328	Cash-save DIY Ltd	16	6 -176 North Street	Should be 166-176 in Address 1 column
000369	D I Y Discount	62 Old Church St	10	10 is meaningless. Delete.
000381	Focus DIY Ltd	Unit 1 Whistleberry Road		Street name should be in Address 2 column
000392	Home & Garden Supplies	11	5 -117 Penshurst Road	Should be 115 −117 in Address 1 column

122

Task 4

In our version of the sheet created for Task 4, all the errors found in Task 3 have been posted.

The recalculation of the Totals is necessary because they have been entered by hand. Here are the errors you should have found.

Code	Name	30	60	90	Original Total	Revised Total	Difference
000028	Rkp Hardware	1052.88	1095.85	5.17	2150.00	2153.90	3.90
000042	Do It All Ltd	843.24	1030.63	339.53	2218.40	2213.40	-5.00
000058	Wasons Paint Paper & D I Y	105.08	73.03	0.39	300.50	178.50	-122.00
000084	Do It All Ltd	67.51	101.27	27.57	916.35	196.35	-720.00
000126	Texas Homecare Ltd	1376.53	1081.56	213.46	2761.55	2671.55	-90.00
000139	Great Mills DIY Superstore	310.55	411.65	3.70	725.09	725.90	0.81
000175	B & Q DIY Supercentre	753.51	723.96	75.48	5112.95	1552.95	-3560.00
000224	M M Patel	923.85	852.79	38.11	184.75	1814.75	1630.00
000241	Homebase Ltd	1169.01	1428.80	2.34	2600.51	2600.15	-0.36
000255	G Langford	507.04	449.64	48.87	1000.00	1005.55	5.55
000284	Decora DIY Superstore	577.41	491.87	0.00	1285.20	1069.28	-215.92
000433	Texas Homecare Ltd	588.24	588.23	55.18	1234.56	1231.65	-2.91
							-3075.93

REPORT

To: Charles Davis
From: Accounting Technician
Date: 3 November 2000

Subject: Aged debtors analyis

As requested, here is a report on the current situation regarding money owed to the company and speed of payment.

The company is presently owed more than half a million ponds by its debtors. Ana analysis of the totals by age gives the following results.

0-30	31-60	61-90	Total
305,618.62	310,756.89	34,880.42	651,255.93
47%	48%	5%	100%

As you can see nearly half of this debt is less than one month old and almost all the rest less than two months. According to this analysis there are no amounts that have been outstanding for more than three months, which is to be expected given that it is supposed to be company policy that such debts are written off.

In the light of this I think the company need have relatively few worries about continuing to be able to finance its overdraft: this is a record of cash collection that should satisfy any bank manager. However, it would be useful to see information on trends in previous months, to see whether the age of debts has increased.

The largest single total outstanding is £2,975, owed by Homebase in Southampton. However there are eleven other accounts owing more than £2,900, thirteen owing over £2, 800, fourteen owing over £2,700 and so on: debts are spread fairly evenly over a range from £12.30 up to £2,975, with no notable clustering around a particular balance.

The largest amount outstanding for over 60 days is £544.99 (Emerys Home Improvements, Solihull). Again these figures are spread broadly across a range upwards from £0.00. Surprisingly only fifteen of the 435 accounts have a nil balance in the over 60 days column. More surprising no customers have a nil balance. This is clearly healthy for business (customers keep on buying) if it is correct, but it is quite unusual.

It is interesting to look at the data if the amounts owed by customers with more than one branch are amalgamated. A list of customers whose branches collectively owe more than £5,000 is presented below.

Predictably the major DIY stores are the biggest debtors. B & Q stores represent the biggest single debtor, owing 12% of the total amount outstanding, or around £80,000. Homebase come next with 7% (over £45,000). Unfortunately we do not have sales turnover information: it would be interesting to know whether B & Q are significantly our biggest customer (and why, if so) or if they are just the slowest payer amongst big customers.

Here are the figures referred to.

Name	Balance	% of Total
B & Q DIY Supercentre	80622.50	12%
Homebase Ltd	45648.40	7%
Do It All Ltd	26245.45	4%
Great Mills DIY Superstore	19426.75	3%
Texas Homecare Ltd	17850.00	3%
Wickes Building Supplies Ltd	12161.80	2%
Fads	11376.40	2%
Focus DIY Ltd	8692.95	1%
Homestyle	4992.05	1%
Do It Yourself Supplies	4777.85	1%
Magnet Ltd	4527.95	1%
Glyn Web	4266.15	1%

Please do not hesitate to ask if there are any specific matters in this report that you would like to investigate in more depth.

Tutorial note. As usual you can use sorting and filtering to derive the above information or else try a Pivot Table if you have that facility. Here is how the information about DIY chain stores was generated.

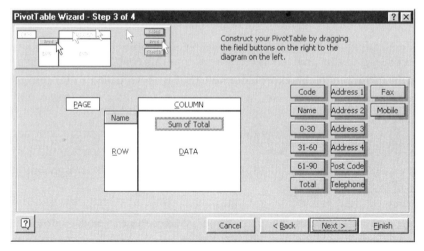

The data in the Pivot Table then had to be selected and sorted, and an additional percentage column was calculated.

Task 6

REPORT

To: Charles Davis
From: Accounting Technician
Date: 3 November 2000

Introduction

As requested this report sets out:

(a)   why the company needs an integrated accounting system;

(b)   what issues need to be considered when transferring data from existing records onto the new system.

Integrated accounting systems

Integrated systems can be formally defined as a number of systems which, although capable of autonomous operation, may be linked closely to form a comprehensive and single view to the user. The use of common files or records by the individual systems is a feature of integration.

In the case of our business for instance sales orders are processed by one system, stock records are kept under another, purchases under another, and production under yet another. Sales depend on stocks being available, and the availability of stocks depends on materials being available and production getting on with making the products. However, if none of the systems con trolling these parts of the business are communicating with each other, no-one will know what is the best thing to do in the interest of the business as a whole.

A good illustration of this was provided in my earlier report about aged debtors: I was able to inform you about the debt position, but not able to relate the information I had to cumulative sales figures because these are not recorded as part of the current system for administering debts, and the information was not available to me.

The diagram below might help to make this clearer. It deals with stock control, sales order and purchases applications.

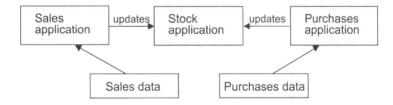

The advantages of integrated processing, therefore, are as follows.

(a)   Each part of the system can be used separately, or in a combination of the parts, or as a total system.

(b)   A transaction item *only has to be entered once* to update all parts of the system. Duplication of effort is avoided, and so is the need to store the same data in several different places (data redundancy).

(c)   Integration of data means that *all departments in a company are using the same information* and inter-departmental disagreements based on differences about 'facts' can be avoided.

(d)   Managers throughout the organisation should have access to fully up-to-date information drawn from sources right across the organisation, not just from one source. This ought to improve the breadth of vision and quality of management decisions.

(e)   Integration will require standardisation and better defined and documented system design. For example it should bring about standard ways of naming files and of constructing spreadsheets.

Transferring data

Having sung the praises of integrated systems, it has to be acknowledged that it is not going to be easy to pull together the various systems now in existence in the company.

Because of the volume of data that must be copied on to the new files, the problem of **input errors** is a serious one, whatever validation checks may be operating.

Once the file has been created, **extensive checking** for accuracy is essential, otherwise considerable problems may arise when the system becomes operational.

Given that the system is already largely computerised, the difficulties of file conversion may be reduced. When it comes to the actual transcription from the old files to the new computer files the use of a special conversion program or translation program will speed up the whole process.

Thus, rather than typing data into records individually, many modern accounting packages have an *import* option that lets you enter data directly from text files generated by other programs, such as spreadsheets and word processors.

There are still a number of issues to address, however.

(a)   Ensuring that the original record files are accurate and up to date. This is exactly what I am doing at present with the debtors records.

(b)   The possible need for additional staff to cope with the file conversion and prevent bottlenecks. Also the need for training of staff in the new system.

(c)   The establishment of cut-off dates where live files are being converted (should the conversion be during slack times, for example, during holidays, weekends?).

(d)   The decision as to whether files should be converted all at once, or whether the conversion should be file by file or record group by record group (with subsequent amalgamation).

There are also several options for the method of actually changing over to the new system.

(a)   Directly: the old system is completely replaced by the new system in one move. This is risky if it is not absolutely certain that the new systems will do all it is intended to do.

(b)   By 'parallel running', which is a form of changeover whereby the old and new systems are run in parallel for a period of time, both processing current data and enabling cross checking to be made.

(c)   On a piecemeal basis, with departments, say, adopting the new system one at a time, so that each benefits from knowledge of the teething problems of the previous department, and the business as a whole is not put at risk. This may be the most sensible approach in our case.

I hope this report has been informative and has given you food for thought. If you would like to discuss any of the issues in more depth I would be happy to do so.

Password

The password to open the BPP solution is **GadGet**

SOLUTION TO TRIAL RUN DEVOLVED ASSESSMENT 6: HARRY ALEXANDER

Solution

For a suggested answer look at the BPP file **DA6_S**. The password to open this spreadsheet is given at the end of this solution.

Task 1

In our solution we have entered the data into columns A to E of a separate sheet as follows.

	A	B	C	D	E	F	G	H	I
1	AH8317	1.01		P001	15.00			**Check**	
2	BX3662	5.94		P002	12.00		AH	8317	8317
3	CZ8997	5.38		P003	12.00		BX	3662	3662
4	DN9569	6.59		P004	12.00		CZ	8997	8997
5	ED2677	8.03		P005	12.00		DN	9569	9569
6	FW4100	0.70		P006	12.00		ED	2677	2677
7	GY2898	0.27		P007	12.00		FW	4100	4100
8	HU2871	4.00		P008	9.60		GY	2898	2898
9	JV7549	4.35		P009	9.60		HU	2871	2871
10	KM6315	8.45		P010	9.60		JV	7549	7549
11	LJ1234	0.66		P011	9.60		KM	6315	6315
12	MT9908	1.14		P012	7.70		LJ	1234	1234
13	NG7732	6.93		P013	7.70		MT	9908	9908
14	PF6023	2.81		P014	7.70		NG	7732	7732
15	QE2207	5.67		P015	7.70		PF	6023	6023
16	RK3583	3.60		P016	7.70		QE	2207	2207
17	TP7325	2.34		P017	7.70		RK	3583	3583
18	UQ7049	1.68		P018	7.70		TP	7325	7325
19	VA1662	1.84		P019	7.70		UQ	7049	7049
20	WL5592	3.29		P020	7.70		VA	1662	1662
21	XC5229	0.59		P021	7.70		WL	5592	5592
22	YR8218	3.44		P022	4.80		XC	5229	5229
23	ZB2520	2.04		P023	4.80		YR	8218	8218
24				P024	3.60		ZB	2520	2520
25	**Check**	80.75			200.60				125237
26									

A good way of checking whether you have entered the data for materials costs and labour rates correctly is to calculate the total of the figures manually from the information given and then sum the figures you have entered in your spreadsheet to see if the two totals agree. Check yours against ours shown above.

The employee numbers can be checked by visual inspection very easily. The materials codes are much more difficult to check. In our answer we have extracted the letters and numbers using the formulae =LEFT(A1,2) in column G, =RIGHT(A1,4) in column H, and =VALUE(H2) in column I. This at least allows you to calculate a total of the four digit numbers in the materials codes. An alternative way of ensuring accuracy might have been to copy the Materials code column, sort it, and then delete duplicates.

Task 2

Here is the answer you should have got. The totals are shown in Row 422 of our answer.

	£
Total materials cost	47,467.33
Total labour cost	35,364.80
	82,832.13

127

The best way to do this is to use the **LOOKUP** function (Lotus 1-2-3 VLOOKUP) in columns E and I. (A slower alternative would be to enter the data line by line, after sorting it by materials code.)

The formulae we use refer to the sheet Task 1 (Lookup) in which we have entered the cost and rate data (see the solution to Task 1). They look up the relevant cost and multiply by the quantity in column D or the hours in column H.

Column E   =D2*LOOKUP(C2,'Task 1 (Lookup)'!\$A\$1:\$B\$23)

Column I   =H2*LOOKUP(F2,'Task 1 (Lookup)'!\$D\$1:\$E\$24)

Make sure you understand this because it is a very useful feature. (If necessary, consult Help in Excel for more details on this function.)

	I2				=H2*LOOKUP(F2,Task 1 (Lookup)'!\$D\$1:\$E\$24)				
	A	B	C	D	E	F	G	H	I
1	Issue note	Job	Materials code	Quantity	Materials Cost	Employee	Job	Labour hours	Labour cost
2	47023	728	AH8317	35	35.35	P002	726	77	924.00
3	47024	732	TP7325	29	67.86	P002	728	67	804.00
4	47025	733	ED2677	51	409.53	P002	732	40	480.00
5	47026	731	QE2207	62	351.54	P003	726	24	288.00
6	47027	731	YR8218	61	209.84	P003	728	40	480.00
7	47028	724	ED2677	57	457.71	P003	731	37	444.00
8	47029	724	PF6023	50	140.50	P003	733	83	996.00
9	47030	726	XC5229	13	7.67	P004	724	42	504.00
10	47031	732	WL5592	13	42.77	P004	727	77	924.00
11	47032	729	RK3583	54	194.40	P004	731	31	372.00
12	47033	729	ZB2520	1	2.04	P004	732	34	408.00
13	47034	728	QE2207	45	255.15	P005	724	68	816.00
14	47035	730	YR8218	15	51.60	P005	727	61	732.00
15	47036	726	GY2898	6	1.62	P005	728	55	660.00
16	47037	729	UQ7049	21	35.28	P006	724	34	408.00
17	47038	729	CZ8997	30	161.40	P006	726	29	348.00
18	47039	729	DN9569	32	210.88	P006	731	79	948.00
19	47040	729	PF6023	53	148.93	P006	732	42	504.00
20	47041	724	TP7325	48	112.32	P007	730	71	852.00
21	47042	730	ZB2520	53	108.12	P007	733	79	948.00
22	47043	732	UQ7049	55	92.40	P007	727	34	408.00
23	47044	732	ZB2520	13	26.52	P008	724	11	105.60
24	47045	727	FW4100	41	28.70	P008	725	62	595.20
25	47046	731	TP7325	50	117.00	P008	726	28	268.80

Task 3

Tutorial note. You can find the information for this task quickly by using Pivot Tables, but it is best to do separate Pivot Tables for materials costs and labour costs, otherwise you may get nonsensical results. Alternatively you can use sorting or filters to extract and sum the information from the main table and successively paste the totals for each job into another sheet. Note that a *chart* of the data is very useful.

REPORT

To: Production Manager
From: Accounting Technician
Date: 5 November 2000

Subject: Job costs, October 2000

Job costs for the month may be summarised as follows. All costs are shown in £'s.

	By job				By total cost		
Job	Total cost	Materials cost	Labour cost	Job	Total cost	Materials cost	Labour cost
724	7,696.35	3,979.65	3,716.70	728	10,112.00	4,809.50	5,302.50
725	7,949.35	5,308.25	2,641.10	732	9,789.85	5,398.15	4,391.70
726	6,763.83	3,580.53	3,183.30	731	9,125.20	5,477.10	3,648.10
727	8,509.91	4,287.41	4,222.50	733	8,900.11	4,586.71	4,313.40
728	10,112.00	4,809.50	5,302.50	727	8,509.91	4,287.41	4,222.50
729	7,507.32	5,763.82	1,743.50	725	7,949.35	5,308.25	2,641.10
730	6,478.21	4,276.21	2,202.00	724	7,696.35	3,979.65	3,716.70
731	9,125.20	5,477.10	3,648.10	729	7,507.32	5,763.82	1,743.50
732	9,789.85	5,398.15	4,391.70	726	6,763.83	3,580.53	3,183.30
733	8,900.11	4,586.71	4,313.40	730	6,478.21	4,276.21	2,202.00
	82,832.13	47,467.33	35,364.80		82,832.13	47,467.33	35,364.80

Job 728 was the most expensive, costing over £10,000 to complete, while Job 730, done at a cost of around £6,500, was the least expensive.

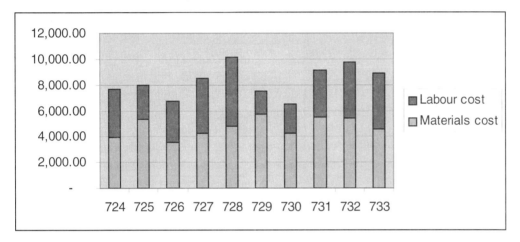

The average cost for all of the ten jobs completed in the month was around £8,250.

A breakdown of costs into labour and materials totals reveals certain matters that may be worthy of further investigation. Most jobs have a materials cost that is only slightly higher than the labour cost, but the following jobs depart from this trend.

(a) Job 729 cost over £5,750 in materials but less than £1,750 in labour.

(b) Job 725 was nearly £3,000 more expensive in terms of materials than labour.

(c) Jobs 730 and 731 were around £2,000 more expensive in terms of materials than labour.

(c) Job 728 cost around £500 more in labour than it did in materials.

Notes and queries for personal use

1   Which jobs were accepted at the standard price of £10,000 and which not? The company will make a loss on job 728, and only a relatively small profit on job 732. If all jobs are priced at £10,000 a mark up of a third is only achieved on three out of ten (726, 729, 730).

2   Can jobs be identified in advance as being particularly labour intensive or materials intensive? If they could be categorised at the outset as, say "L" jobs for labour intensive, or "M" jobs for materials intensive, this might be useful, both for planning in the personnel and purchasing departments, and for later analysis.

3   How is work allocated between staff? Some staff are paid considerably more than others, and this may have a bearing on costs incurred. On the other hand, salaries/wages may be fixed costs.

4   Do labour and materials costs change from month to month? If not this data could be incorporated permanently into a spreadsheet model rather than having to be re-entered and carefully checked each time.

5   Can I be sure that all the figures for quantities and hours have been entered accurately?

Tutorial note. Many points could be made here. Marks should be awarded for valid comments of any kind. The spreadsheet upon which the information provided in the report is based will be found in the BPP file DA6_S. This was originally generated using Pivot Tables for Materials cost and then again for Labour cost (see the sheet Task 3 (Pivot) for a sample based on cells **B1 to E421 only** of the main spreadsheet).

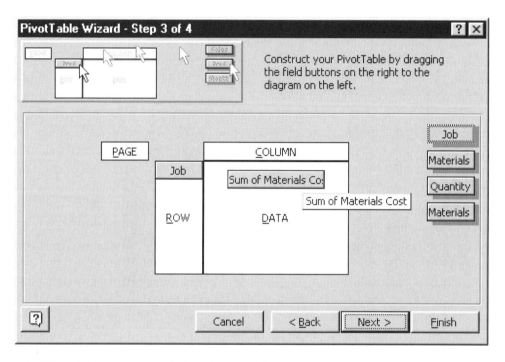

The data from the Pivot Tables was copied and pasted into another sheet, summed, and then copied again and sorted by total cost. The final sheet is reproduced below in 'formula' format.

	A	B	C	D	E	F	G	H	I	J
1	Job	Total cost	Materials cost	Labour cost			Job	Total cost	Materials cost	Labour cost
2	724	=SUM(C2:D2)	3979.65	3716.7			728	=SUM(I2:J2)	4809.5	5302.5
3	725	=SUM(C3:D3)	5308.25	2641.1			732	=SUM(I3:J3)	5398.15	4391.7
4	726	=SUM(C4:D4)	3580.53	3183.3			731	=SUM(I4:J4)	5477.1	3648.1
5	727	=SUM(C5:D5)	4287.41	4222.5			733	=SUM(I5:J5)	4586.71	4313.4
6	728	=SUM(C6:D6)	4809.5	5302.5			727	=SUM(I6:J6)	4287.41	4222.5
7	729	=SUM(C7:D7)	5763.82	1743.5			725	=SUM(I7:J7)	5308.25	2641.1
8	730	=SUM(C8:D8)	4276.21	2202			724	=SUM(I8:J8)	3979.65	3716.7
9	731	=SUM(C9:D9)	5477.1	3648.1			729	=SUM(I9:J9)	5763.82	1743.5
10	732	=SUM(C10:D10)	5398.15	4391.7			726	=SUM(I10:J10)	3580.53	3183.3
11	733	=SUM(C11:D11)	4586.71	4313.4			730	=SUM(I11:J11)	4276.21	2202
12		=SUM(B2:B11)	=SUM(C2:C11)	=SUM(D2:D11)				=SUM(H2:H11)	=SUM(I2:I11)	=SUM(J2:J11)
13										
14		Maximum	Job 728	=MAX(B2:B11)						
15		Minimum	Job 730	=MIN(B2:B11)						
16		Average	of all jobs	=AVERAGE(B2:B11)						

The chart is produced by selecting the Materials cost and Labour cost data and specifying the Job number data as the Category X axis labels.

Task 4

Tutorial note. To complete this task the data for Job 718 needs to be entered in a spreadsheet and the data for Job 730 needs to be extracted from the main spreadsheet. the two sets of data can then be compared with a simple 'column A minus column B' type formula.

The material TP7325 data can be extracted by sorting the main spreadsheet on the relevant column.

REPORT

To: Production Manager
From: Accounting Technician
Date: 5 November 2000

Subject: Materials usage, October 2000

Jobs 718 and 730

As requested, the table below shows a summary of the differences in material usage between Job 718 and Job 730.

Material	718	730	Difference
AH8317	7	7	0
BX3662	36	36	0
CZ8997	40	42	2
DN9569	22	60	38
ED2677	80	79	-1
FW4100	42		-42
GY2898			0
HU2871	5	5	0
JV7549	62	65	3
KM6315	70	72	2
LJ1234	75	75	0
MT9908	40	41	1
NG7732	60	59	-1
PF6023	124	113	-11
QE2207	10	12	2
RK3583	50	57	7
TP7325			0
UQ7049	80	82	2
VA1662		42	42
WL5592	34	34	0
XC5229			0
YR8218	47	47	0
ZB2520	149	149	0
	1033	1077	44

The following points may be noticed.

(a) Job 730 used more materials overall than job 718, though not significantly more so. This is largely accounted for by the fact that Job 730 used 38 more units of DN9569 than Job 718.

(b) Materials FW4100 and VA1662 may be interchangeable: Job 718 used 42 units of FW4100 while Job 730 used none. Job 730 used 42 units of VA1662 while Job 718 used none.

(c) Materials GY2898, TP7325 and XC5229 were not used by either job.

(d) All other differences are negligible.

Material TP7325

Usage of material TP7325 was distributed between jobs as follows.

Job	Total
724	48
725	37
726	47
727	49
728	97
729	14
731	50
732	44
733	91
Total	477

The average amount used was 53 units, although this was distorted by two much higher values (Jobs 728 and 733), and one much lower value (Job 729). If this data is removed the average is about 46 units, slightly below your expectations. However, with the exceptions noted, usage was broadly the same across all Jobs.

Overall, usage was down in October 2000 from 520 units in September to 477 in October. This is perhaps because material TP7325 was not used for Job 730 at all, according to issue note records.

Task 5

NOTE

To: Production Manager
From: Accounting Technician
Date: 5 November 2000

Subject: Labour hours, October 2000

Job 728 took longest, at 585 hours, while job 729 took the least time, at less than half of this (221 hours). A full analysis of jobs in order of time spent is shown below.

Job	Hours
728	585
732	473
733	448
727	439
724	427
731	368
725	336
726	327
730	240
729	221

The longest time spent by a single employee on one job was 89 hours, taken by employee P014 on Job 729.

All employees worked 184 hours during the month apart from employees P001, P023 and P024, none of whom appear to have worked on jobs at all during the month.

Tutorial note. The illustration below shows how the data required for this answer might be derived by a combination of a pivot table and simple formulae and sorting.

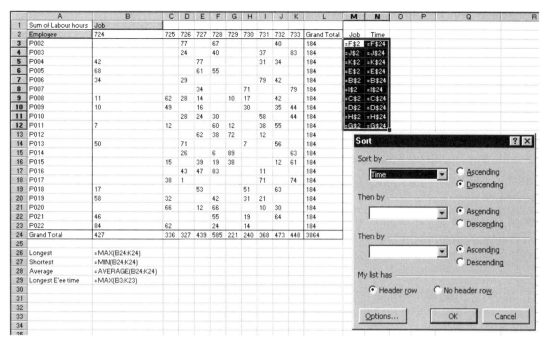

Task 6

REPORT

To: Production Manager
From: Accounting Technician
Date: 7 November 2000

Subject: Using Information Technology at Harry Alexander Ltd

Introduction

This report discusses the implications of introducing more automation to the production department job costing function and considers the possible benefits to the company as a whole of a system that enables more group working and information sharing.

Job costing

At present this is done using a spreadsheet into which details of issue notes and labour hours are entered manually from the original paper-based documents. This has two main disadvantages.

(a)   It is extremely time consuming.

(b)   It is prone to error.

In the long term I would suggest that the company invests in a job costing 'module', preferably one that can link up with the financial accounting system. However, this needs to be discussed with all the staff involved and probably also with the company's auditors. Even if we do agree that this would be desirable it will still take some time to identify a suitable package, install it and train users.

In the mean time, however, there are a number of improvements that could be made to the current system.

(a)   Instead of filling in pre-printed issue notes by hand the details could be entered directly into a spreadsheet model. Modern spreadsheet packages are programmable to some extent and it ought to be fairly easy to devise a series of 'macros' that would meet both the task of keeping proper control and proper records and providing data for subsequent analysis.

This would cut out a whole stage of costing work, saving a considerable amount of time and significantly reducing the likelihood of errors.

(b) Better still, the data could be entered into a database. With modern packages such as Microsoft Access it is possible even for a novice to devise professional looking entry screens and output reports.

(c) In either case it would be possible to cost materials issues at the time of issue, rather than waiting until the end of the month, cutting out a further stage of the task.

(d) Details of labour hours could be dealt with and costed in a similar way, although issues arise of who would enter the data (individual employees? a production supervisor?) and how many computers would be needed. There are sophisticated time recording systems available, but these are expensive and probably go beyond the present needs of the company.

I need to gain a better understanding of the way in which work is allocated to employees and how employees manage their time before making a firm recommendation in this area.

Networked PCs

At present the company operates stand-alone PCs, that is PCs that are not connected up to one another. However, most companies of any size these days are finding it advantageous to set up networks of interconnected PCs with a powerful 'server' PC running jointly used services such as e-mail and printing. There are a number of reasons for this, including the following.

(a) *Shared work-loads.* Each PC in a network can do the same work. If there are separate stand-alone PCs, A might do job 1, B might do job 2, C might do job 3 and so on. In a network, any PC, (A, B or C) could do any job (1, 2 or 3). This provides flexibility in sharing work-loads. In a peak period for job 1, say, two or more people can share the work without having to leave their own desk.

(b) *Shared programs and data.* Program and data files held on a file server can be shared by all the PCs in the network. With stand-alone PCs, each computer would have its own data files, and there might be unnecessary duplication of data.

A system where everyone uses the same data will help to improve data processing and decision making. The value of some information increases with its availability.

(c) *Shared peripherals.* Peripheral equipment can be shared. For example, five PCs might share a single on-line printer, whereas if there were stand-alone PCs, each might be given its own separate printer. If resources are scarce (for example fast laser printers) this is a significant benefit.

(d) *Greater resilience.* Processing is spread over several computers, so 'client/server' systems are more resilient. If one server breaks down, other locations can carry on processing.

(e) *Communication and time management.* LANs can be linked up to the office communications network, thus adding to the processing capabilities in an office. Electronic mail can be used to send messages, memos and electronic letters from node to node. Electronic calendar and diary facilities can also be used.

There are of course some disadvantages.

(a) It is easier to control and maintain a system centrally. In particular it is easier to keep data secure.

(b) Duplication of data may be a problem if individual users do not follow a disciplined approach.

(c) A network requires investment in computer hardware and cabling and also in software such as a network operating system, e-mail and fax software and so on.

(d) Ideally the system needs someone fairly expert to administer it. It will be very frustrating for users if they are not able to do simple day to day tasks that they used be able to do perfectly well on their stand-alone PCs, simply because nobody knows how the server works.

I hope this has given you some insight into the issues that you were interested in. I should be glad to provide any other information you may require.

Password

The password to open the BPP solution is **Caustic**

SOLUTION TO TRIAL RUN DEVOLVED ASSESSMENT 7: HANDLEY INSURANCE

Solution

For a suggested answer look at the BPP file **DA7_S**. The password to open this spreadsheet is given at the end of this solution.

Task 1

The columns need resizing to accommodate all the information they hold and their headings should be emphasised by formatting. Some of the information looks better if it is centred. Some numbers are incorrectly aligned, for instance in rows 166 to 173, 251, 303, 313, 320, and 362. Money amounts should be stated to two decimal places. The sheet should be renamed as something like **Handley Insurance – Fixed Assets**. (In our answer, however, for the sake of clarity, we have named the revised version after the tasks it answers.)

You might have been concerned at the inconsistent use of capitals and lower case for entries, but it is probably not worth spending too much time changing this.

The following two illustrations show how a revised version might look.

	A	B	C	D	E	F	G
1	Date	Code	Description 1	Description 2	Description 3	Serial number	Location/Employee
2	02-Jun-1994	1	50 FILING CABINETS (SECOND HAND)	52" High 16" Wide 24.5"	4 Drawer Non - Locking	n/a	Handley House
3	02-Jun-1994	2	DESK	1200x800x720	18mm top	DE880/68579	Handley House
4	02-Jun-1994	3	DESK	1200x800x720	18mm top	DE880/41773	Handley House
5	02-Jun-1994	4	TASK CHAIR	GAS LIFT/LOW BACK	Without arms	T10-8860	Handley House
6	02-Jun-1994	5	TASK CHAIR	GAS LIFT/LOW BACK	Without arms	T10-5466	Handley House
7	05-Jun-1994	6	TASK CHAIR	GAS LIFT/LOW BACK	Without arms	T10-6379	Handley House
8	05-Jun-1994	7	TASK CHAIR	GAS LIFT/LOW BACK	Without arms	T10-4567	Handley House
9	05-Jun-1994	8	TASK CHAIR	GAS LIFT/LOW BACK	Without arms	T10-6923	Handley House
10	05-Jun-1994	9	DESK	1200x800x720	18mm top	DE880/43672	Handley House
11	06-Jun-1994	10	TASK CHAIR	GAS LIFT/LOW BACK	Without arms	T10-6773	Handley House
12	06-Jun-1994	11	DESK	1200x800x720	18mm top	DE880/53832	Handley House
13	06-Jun-1994	12	DESK	1200x800x720	18mm top	DE880/40375	Handley House
14	07-Jun-1994	13	DESK	1200x800x720	18mm top	DE880/45322	Handley House
15	07-Jun-1994	14	DESK	1200x800x720	18mm top	DE880/45438	Handley House
16	07-Jun-1994	15	HIGH BACK MANAGERS CHAIR	SYNCHRONOUS ACTION	With arms	T66A-2750	Handley House
17	07-Jun-1994	16	HIGH BACK MANAGERS CHAIR	SYNCHRONOUS ACTION	With arms	T66A-1048	Handley House
18	07-Jun-1994	17	HIGH BACK MANAGERS CHAIR	SYNCHRONOUS ACTION	With arms	T66A-2999	Handley House
19	08-Jun-1994	18	DESK	1200x800x720	18mm top	DE880/42995	Handley House
20	09-Jun-1994	19	TASK CHAIR	GAS LIFT/LOW BACK	Without arms	T10-9012	Handley House
21	09-Jun-1994	20	DESK	1200x800x720	18mm top	DE880/79803	Handley House
22	09-Jun-1994	21	DESK	1200x800x720	18mm top	DE880/91110	Handley House
23	10-Jun-1994	23	TASK CHAIR	GAS LIFT/LOW BACK	Without arms	T10-8916	Handley House
24	02-Jul-1994	24	TASK CHAIR	GAS LIFT/LOW BACK	Without arms	T10-4404	Handley House
25	15-Dec-1994	28	DESK	1200x800x720	18mm top	DE880/27491	Handley House
26	15-Dec-1994	29	DESK	1200x800x720	18mm top	DE880/88150	Handley House
27	15-Dec-1994	30	DESK	1200x800x720	18mm top	DE880/28203	Handley House
28	15-Dec-1994	31	DESK	1200x800x720	18mm top	DE880/28203	Handley House
29	15-Dec-1994	32	DESK	1200x800x720	25mm top	DE885/67807	Handley House
30	04-Jun-1995	34	DESK	1200x800x720	25mm top	DE885/33890	Handley House
31	04-Jun-1995	35	DESK	1200x800x720	25mm top	DE885/31728	Handley House
32	04-Jun-1995	36	DESK	1200x800x720	25mm top	DE885/32728	Handley House
33	04-Jun-1995	37	DESK	1200x000x720	25mm top	DE885/48930	Handley House
34	04-Jun-1995	38	DESK	1200x800x720	25mm top	DE885/41623	Handley House
35	04-Jun-1995	39	DESK	1200x800x720	25mm top	DE885/15128	Handley House

	H	I	J	K	L	M	N	O
1	Supplier	Asset Category	Department	Depn method	Depn rate	Cost price	Depn to date	Book value
2		FF	0	S	0.1	625.00	350.00	275.00
3	Davis Office Supplies	FF	0	S	0.1	199.00	111.44	87.56
4	Davis Office Supplies	FF	0	S	0.1	199.00	111.44	87.56
5	ErgoFurn	FF		S	0.1	91.00	50.96	40.04
6	ErgoFurn	FF		S	0.1	91.00	50.96	40.04
7	ErgoFurn	FF		S	0.1	91.00	50.96	40.04
8	ErgoFurn	FF		S	0.1	91.00	50.96	40.04
9	ErgoFurn	FF		S	0.1	91.00	50.96	40.04
10	Davis Office Supplies	FF	0	S	0.1	199.00	111.44	87.56
11	ErgoFurn	FF		S	0.1	91.00	50.96	40.04
12	Davis Office Supplies	FF	0	S	0.1	199.00	111.44	87.56
13	Davis Office Supplies	FF	0	S	0.1	199.00	111.44	87.56
14	Davis Office Supplies	FF	0	S	0.1	199.00	111.44	87.56
15	Davis Office Supplies	FF	0	S	0.1	199.00	111.44	87.56
16	ErgoFurn	FF		S	0.1	178.00	99.68	78.32
17	ErgoFurn	FF		S	0.1	178.00	99.68	78.32
18	ErgoFurn	FF		S	0.1	178.00	99.68	78.32
19	Davis Office Supplies	FF	0	S	0.1	199.00	111.44	87.56
20	ErgoFurn	FF		S	0.1	91.00	50.96	40.04
21	Davis Office Supplies	FF	0	S	0.1	199.00	111.44	87.56
22	Davis Office Supplies	FF	0	S	0.1	199.00	111.44	87.56
23	ErgoFurn	FF		S	0.1	91.00	50.96	40.04
24	ErgoFurn	FF		S	0.1	91.00	50.05	40.95
25	Davis Office Supplies	FF	0	S	0.1	199.00	99.50	99.50
26	Davis Office Supplies	FF	0	S	0.1	199.00	99.50	99.50
27	Davis Office Supplies	FF	0	S	0.1	199.00	99.50	99.50
28	Davis Office Supplies	FF	0	S	0.1	199.00	99.50	99.50
29	Davis Office Supplies	FF	0	S	0.1	209.00	104.50	104.50
30	Davis Office Supplies	FF	0	S	0.1	209.00	96.14	112.86
31	Davis Office Supplies	FF	0	S	0.1	209.00	96.14	112.86
32	Davis Office Supplies	FF	0	S	0.1	209.00	96.14	112.86
33	Davis Office Supplies	FF	0	S	0.1	209.00	96.14	112.86
34	Davis Office Supplies	FF	0	S	0.1	209.00	96.14	112.86
35	Davis Office Supplies	FF	0	S	0.1	209.00	96.14	112.86

Given the width of the spreadsheet it is useful to split the screen and freeze the panes (at cell C2) to make it easier to move about the spreadsheet without getting lost.

Task 2

You should have discovered at this point that the data as originally provided is **not sorted in date or code order** (in fact it is sorted by asset category).

Your first task, therefore is to re-sort the data. The last entry should then be dated 10 Oct 2000 (code number 415). The first new code number should be 416.

Here is our answer, also showing the last item in the re-sorted spreadsheet. Make sure you had the asset category, and depreciation rate and method correct. If there were any items that you were unsure of, for instance the 'Lift (gas)', you should have searched the spreadsheet for one or other of these words, or for the name of the supplier, to discover that it is actually a type of chair. Similarly with the 'screen'.

	A	B	C	D	E	F	G
1	Date purchased	Code	Description 1	Description 2	Description 3	Serial number	Location/Employee
416	10-Oct-00	415	PROTEUS MMX 12.1" TFT	233 MHz	Laptop		
417	20-Oct-00	416	PRINTER	LEXUS LASER 353			
418	01-Nov-00	417	FORD ESCORT 1.6	BLUE METALLIC		R452 PJX	
419	17-Nov-00	418	CHAIR	GAS LIFT		JX-4713	
420	05-Dec-00	419	PC-PENTIUM	400 MHz		CQ4-521389	
421	05-Dec-00	420	SCREEN				

	G	H	I	J	K	L	M
1	Location/Employee	Supplier	Asset Category	Department	Depn method	Depn rate	Cost price
416			OM		S	0.33	1325.00
417		Simply Computers	OM		S	0.33	649.00
418		Harwoods	V		R	0.25	8995.00
419		ErgoFurn	FF		S	0.1	143.99
420		Compaq	OM		S	0.33	1854.99
421			FF		S	0.1	185.00

No entries are made in columns N and O yet. Note that the screen referred to is a partition, not a computer VDU. See our version of the memo that we asked you to write for further points.

MEMO

To: Peter Worthington
From: Accounting Technician
Date: 4 January 2001

Subject: Fixed Assets

Thank you for picking out invoices for items that need to be included in the fixed assets schedule. I am returning the invoices for the following items.

Desk lamp   We do not capitalise items costing less than £50. This invoice should be posted to an expense account.

Microsoft Office 97   Computer software is not normally capitalised.

I am retaining the invoice for the Sanyo Playstation, which does not appear to be a valid business asset. I note it was bought on Christmas Eve. This will be followed up with Sarah Handley.

Could you please let me have a note of the serial number of the Lexus Laser printer purchased on 20 October 2000. This is important information, especially for easily portable items, and would be needed for insurance purposes in the event of a burglary.

Task 3

The following items should have been picked out as unusual in this business context. Some may indeed be valid items, for example the compant may have a gymnasium. These could be discovered fairly quickly by sorting or filtering the spreadsheet. The supplier Argos in the previous task was intended to be both a clue and a distraction (for instance the company bought a TV and video at Argos, but these are quite legitimate business items for training and news purposes.)

114	HAIRDRYER ON STAND	Finish Beauty Products
187	DELTA METEOR	Sportsworld
262	GARDEN SHED	Argos
383	BODY SOLARIUM	Argos
406	WEIDER VIPER GYM	Sportsworld

The following items should not have been capitalised (according to the company's fixed asset policy), because they cost less than £50. Arguably this also applies to the 50 filing cabinets (Asset 1) which originally cost £12.50 each, but we have let these remain in the records.

Code	Description 1	Cost price
45	DESK LAMP	12.90
78	DESK LAMP	12.90
188	MILLENIUM KETTLE	36.40
198	TOASTER	39.25
333	FAN	24.75
337	FAN	24.75
339	FAN	24.75
340	FAN	24.75
342	FAN	24.75
351	DESK LAMP	12.90
412	DESK LAMP	12.90

The following items have identical serial numbers and have probably been entered twice.

30	DE880/28203
31	DE880/28203
68	DE1280/7559
72	DE1280/7559
145	DE1880/425
167	DE1880/425
146	T10A-8904
168	T10A-8904

You can track these down by copying the code and serial number columns into a separate sheet, sorting by serial number, and then using a formula in an adjacent column as in the illustration below. (This spreadsheet was created temporarily for the purpose of this task and is not included in the BPP solution file.)

	A	B	C
190	68	DE1280/7559	=IF(B190=B189,"Error",0)
191	72	DE1280/7559	=IF(B191=B190,"Error",0)
192	50	DE1280/7578	=IF(B192=B191,"Error",0)
193	47	DE1280/7671	=IF(B193=B192,"Error",0)
194	86	DE1280/7843	=IF(B194=B193,"Error",0)
195	51	DE1280/9234	=IF(B195=B194,"Error",0)
196	48	DE1280/9485	=IF(B196=B195,"Error",0)
197	82	DE1280/9750	=IF(B197=B196,"Error",0)
198	177	DE1880/168	=IF(B198=B197,"Error",0)
199	179	DE1880/202	=IF(B199=B198,"Error",0)
200	141	DE1880/268	=IF(B200=B199,"Error",0)
201	149	DE1880/271	=IF(B201=B200,"Error",0)
202	153	DE1880/321	=IF(B202=B201,"Error",0)
203	139	DE1880/365	=IF(B203=B202,"Error",0)
204	135	DE1880/397	=IF(B204=B203,"Error",0)
205	163	DE1880/415	=IF(B205=B204,"Error",0)
206	145	DE1880/425	=IF(B206=B205,"Error",0)
207	167	DE1880/425	=IF(B207=B206,"Error",0)
208	161	DE1880/436	=IF(B208=B207,"Error",0)
209	90	DE1880/445	=IF(B209=B208,"Error",0)
210	157	DE1880/486	=IF(B210=B209,"Error",0)

Other points that are worth making are as follows.

(a) Many of the descriptions of similar assets are entered in an inconsistent way. This is possibly inevitable given the size of the spreadsheet and the fact that it has probably been compiled by different people over a long period.

(b) Many fields are blank, notably in the supplier name, location and department columns.

MEMO

To: Sarah Handley
From: Accounting Technician
Date: 4 January 2001

Subject: Fixed Assets

I have been asked to examine and update the company's fixed assets records.

As part of this exercise I need to verify that all assets on the fixed asset register do exist.

Could you please confirm that the following items, which are included in the fixed assets records, are assets used by the company.

Date purchased	Code per assets schedule	Description 1	Description 2	Supplier	Cost price
16-Jul-1996	114	Hairdryer on stand	Babyliss 889 "Superhood"	Finish Beauty Products	54.50
08-May-1997	187	Delta Meteor	Magnetic exercise cycle	Sportsworld	199.00
28-May-1997	262	Garden shed	2.44 x 1.83	Argos	248.50
19-Feb-1999	383	Body solarium	Trilec Model 650	Argos	349.00
14-Jun-2000	406	Weider Viper Gym		Sportsworld	349.99

Tutorial note. The tone of your memo needs to be businesslike but diplomatic. It is possible that these items have been fraudulently 'put through the company books', but they may be genuine mistakes. An added incentive not to offend is that Sarah Handley is a senior member of staff and is married to the Managing Director!

The following assets have been deleted in our solution to Task 3.

Code	Code	Code
31	187	340
45	188	342
68	198	351
78	262	383
114	333	406
167	337	412
168	339	

Task 4

The first job is to extract the data relating to vehicles. You can do this quickly by sorting the spreadsheet from Task 3 by asset category, selecting all the assets with a V category and pasting your selection into a fresh sheet. You do not need all the columns so you can delete all except those shown in the following extract.

BPP
PUBLISHING

	A	B	C	D	E	F
1	Date purchased	Code	Description 1	Cost price	Depn to date per ledger	Book value 1.1.2000 per ledger
2	02-Jul-94	25	BMW 730I SE	43735.00	29040.00	14695.00
3	05-Jul-94	26	CARINA E 1.6 GLI AUTO	24235.34	19240.34	4995.00
4	11-Feb-95	33	AUDI 80 TDI	34682.77	26187.77	8495.00
5	01-Aug-96	115	JAGUAR XJ12	53450.00	45688.77	7761.23
6	29-Nov-96	119	PASSAT 2.0 GL ESTATE	24313.28	14318.28	9995.00
7	02-Jan-97	120	CAVALIER 1.8 CLASSIC	11840.00	6845.00	4995.00
8	08-Jan-97	121	SAAB 9000I CSE EICOE 2.0 TURBO AUTO	27079.30	15589.30	11490.00
9	24-Jan-97	122	AUDI A8 2.8 AUTO SALOON	36595.00	10600.00	25995.00
10	21-Feb-97	123	ROVER 111S	11372.61	6377.61	4995.00
11	23-Feb-97	124	ROVER 218 STDI TURBO DIESEL	17015.59	9520.59	7495.00
12	28-Feb-97	125	SAAB 900S COUPE	21720.56	12125.56	9595.00
13	03-Mar-97	126	DISCOVERY TDI	30472.66	16972.66	13500.00
14	03-Apr-97	127	GOLF CL 1.6	21606.58	11811.58	9795.00
15	15-Apr-97	128	GOLF L	16390.98	8895.98	7495.00
16	21-Apr-97	129	PEUGEOT 306 XRD 1.9	13035.38	7040.38	5995.00
17	22-May-97	244	ALFA ROMEO CLOVER LEAF 24V	29557.27	15607.27	13950.00

The next task is to work out the depreciation in the first year of ownership. The company's depreciation policy specifies that 'A full month's depreciation is provided in the month of purchase (ie an asset bought on, say, 15 July is depreciated at 6/12 times the standard rate in the first year)... '. We therefore need to work out what fraction of a year's depreciation to provide.

There are only 37 vehicles to deal with so you could do this manually. However, one alternative (of several) is to insert a December date in, say, column G, and then subtract the month in column G from the month in column A in the next column, using the **MONTH** function. You then need to add 1, since the spreadsheet does not count one of the months in its subtraction. You can see by inspection in the illustration below that this gives the right answer.

	A	G	H
1	Date purchased	Control	Months
2	02-Jul-94	31-Dec	=(MONTH(G2)-MONTH(A2))+1
3	05-Jul-94	31-Dec	6
4	11-Feb-95	31-Dec	11
5	01-Aug-96	31-Dec	5
6	29-Nov-96	31-Dec	2
7	02-Jan-97	31-Dec	12
8	08-Jan-97	31-Dec	12
9	24-Jan-97	31-Dec	12
10	21-Feb-97	31-Dec	11
11	23-Feb-97	31-Dec	11
12	28-Feb-97	31-Dec	11
13	03-Mar-97	31-Dec	10
14	03-Apr-97	31-Dec	9
15	15-Apr-97	31-Dec	9
16	21-Apr-97	31-Dec	9

To calculate depreciation in the first year, a formula is then needed in column I as follows:

$$=D2*-0.25*H2/12$$

This refers to cost price, the depreciation rate and the fraction of the year, as shown below. Note that we make the figure negative (- 0.25), since we know we are going to be subtracting depreciation.

	A	B	C	D	H	I
1	Date purchased	Code	Description 1	Cost price	Months	1st year
2	02-Jul-94	25	BMW 730I SE	43735.00	6	=D2*-0.25*H2/12
3	05-Jul-94	26	CARINA E 1.6 GLI AUTO	24235.34	6	-3029.42
4	11-Feb-95	33	AUDI 80 TDI	34682.77	11	-7948.13
5	01-Aug-96	115	JAGUAR XJ12	53450.00	5	-5567.71
6	29-Nov-96	119	PASSAT 2.0 GL ESTATE	24313.28	2	-1013.05
7	02-Jan-97	120	CAVALIER 1.8 CLASSIC	11840.00	12	-2960.00
8	08-Jan-97	121	SAAB 9000I CSE EICOE 2.0 TURBO AUTO	27079.30	12	-6769.83
9	24-Jan-97	122	AUDI A8 2.8 AUTO SALOON	36595.00	12	-9148.75
10	21-Feb-97	123	ROVER 111S	11372.61	11	-2606.22

The next step is to calculate the amount brought forward at the beginning of the year after purchase and to calculate depreciation for that year. This may seem a bit laborious, but in fact much of it can be done by filling in cells by dragging with the mouse once the first purchase in a year is done. The illustration below shows the approach we have used.

	B	C	D	H	I	J	K	L	M	N	O	P	Q
1	Code	D	Cost price	Months	1st year	1995 b/f	1995 Depn	1996 b/f	1996 Depn	1997 b/f	1997 Depn	1998 b/f	1998 Depn
2	25	E	43735.00	6	-5466.88	38268.13	-9567.03	28701.09	-7175.27	21525.82	-5381.46	16144.37	-4036.09
3	26	C	24235.34	6	-3029.42	21205.92	-5301.48	15904.44	-3976.11	11928.33	-2982.08	8946.25	-2236.56
4	33	A	34682.77	11	-7948.13			26734.64	-6683.66	20050.98	-5012.74	15038.23	-3759.56
5	115	J	53450.00	5	-5567.71					47882.29	-11970.57	35911.72	-8977.93
6	119	P	24313.28	2	-1013.05					23300.23	-5825.06	17475.17	-4368.79
7	120	C	11840.00	12	-2960.00	=D2+I2		=0.25*J2				8880.00	-2220.00
8	121	S	27079.30	12	-6769.83							20309.48	-5077.37
9	122	A	36595.00	12	-9148.75				=D6+I6			27446.25	-6861.56
10	123	R	11372.61	11	-2606.22							8766.39	-2191.60
11	124	R	17015.59	11	-3899.41							13116.18	-3279.05
12	125	S	21720.56	11	-4977.63						=0.25*N6	16742.93	-4185.73
13	126	D	30472.66	10	-6348.47							24124.19	-6031.05
14	127	C	21606.58	9	-4051.23							17555.35	-4388.84
15	128	C	16390.98	9	-3073.31							13317.67	-3329.42
16	129	P	13035.38	9	-2444.13							10591.25	-2647.81
17	244	A	29557.27	8	-4926.21							24631.06	-6157.76
18	287	G	18359.01	6	-2294.88							16064.13	-4016.03
19	290	P	12039.73	6	-1504.97							10534.76	-2633.69
20	292	C	26994.50	5	-2811.93							24182.57	-6045.64
21	311	T	24999.00	12	-6249.75								
22	312	R	9922.60	12	-2480.65								
23	313	V	17946.05	12	-4486.51								
24	315	V	11231.70	10	-2339.94								
25	316	R	14804.25	9	-2775.80								

Next you need to work out cumulative depreciation by summing the 'Depreciation' columns, not forgetting to include first year depreciation. Here is a full schedule against which to check your own figures.

Code	Description 1	Cumulative 1999	Cumulative 2000
25	BMW 730I SE	-34653.79	-36924.10
26	CARINA E 1.6 GLI AUTO	-19203.08	-20461.14
33	AUDI 80 TDI	-26223.76	-28338.52
115	JAGUAR XJ12	-33249.66	-38299.74
119	PASSAT 2.0 GL ESTATE	-14483.50	-16940.94
120	CAVALIER 1.8 CLASSIC	-6845.00	-8093.75
121	SAAB 9000I CSE EICOE 2.0 TURBO AUTO	-15655.22	-18511.24
122	AUDI A8 2.8 AUTO SALOON	-21156.48	-25016.11
123	ROVER 111S	-6441.52	-7674.29
124	ROVER 218 STDI TURBO DIESEL	-9637.74	-11482.20
125	SAAB 900S COUPE	-12302.66	-14657.14
126	DISCOVERY TDI	-16902.80	-20295.27
127	GOLF CL 1.6	-11731.70	-14200.42
128	GOLF L	-8899.79	-10772.59
129	PEUGEOT 306 XRD 1.9	-7077.80	-8567.20
244	ALFA ROMEO CLOVER LEAF 24V	-15702.30	-19166.04
287	GOLF 1.4 CL	-9322.93	-11581.95
290	PROTON 1.6 SEI PERSONA	-6113.93	-7595.38
292	GOLF GTI 16V	-13391.80	-16792.48
311	TOYOTA COLORADO 1996 P REG	-10937.06	-14452.55
312	ROVER 111 GSI	-4341.14	-5736.50
313	VAUXHALL TIGRA 1.4I	-7851.40	-10375.06
315	VAUXHALL ASTRA 1.6 PREMIER	-4562.88	-6230.08
316	RENAULT LAGUNA 3.0 V6	-5782.91	-8038.25
324	ROVER 416I	-4479.23	-6345.58
325	VAUXHALL VECTRA 1.8 GLS SALOON	-4156.44	-5888.28
326	NISSAN PRIMERA 1.6 LX	-3552.00	-5032.00
332	GOLF GTI 16V	-9701.15	-14024.49
334	MERCEDES BENZ C180 ELEGANCE	-10532.43	-15226.22
336	GOLF 1.4 SE	-5435.13	-7857.31
338	ROVER 214 SI	-4692.51	-6932.11
349	ROVER 420 SI SPORT	-3612.66	-6322.16
388	MERCEDES BENZ C180 ELEGANCE	-6716.33	-12364.15
390	SAAB 900S CONVERTIBLE	-5630.47	-10365.19
391	PEUGEOT 306 GTI 2.0	-3021.72	-6798.88
397	RENAULT LAGUNA 2.0 RT	-702.83	-3338.42
417	FORD ESCORT 1.6		-374.79

A summary schedule is now needed for sending to the auditors. It is best to prepare this on a separate sheet, and use cell references to the previous sheet.

Meat Parwick
24 Apple Road
London
N12 3PP

4 January 2001

Dear Sir / Madam

Handley Insurance: Motor Vehicle Depreciation

In response to your letter of 14 October 2000 concerning Motor Vehicle Depreciation I have recalculated depreciation on all Motor Vehicles.

This exercsise has shown that many of the opening book values as at 1/1/2000 stated in the company's fixed assets records were incorrect.

I have not had the opportunity to discuss this with the person or persons who calculated the original figures. I suspect that the figures were derived from a trade manual to reflect mileage and vehicle specifications.

Most of the difference is accounted for by relatively few vehicles. In one case a vehicle is stated in the books at a figure that is nearly £12,500 less than the figure obtained by applying the company's stated depreciation policy. In another the net book value of a vehicle is stated over £10,500 more than the correctly calculated value.

In total, vehicle assets at the start of the financial year were overstated by £13,268 or 3.5% of net book value. Most vehicles were only over- or understated by a few hundred pounds. A full schedule is enclosed.

I should be grateful for your further advice on how this matter will be dealt with in the financial statements for the year ended 31 December 2000.

Yours faithfully

Accounting Technician

Schedule of fixed asset discrepancies

	A	B	C	D	E	F	G	H	I
1	Date purchased	Code	Description 1	Cost price	Depn	NBV @ 1.1.2000	Original NBV @ 1.1.2000	Difference	%
2	02-Jul-94	25	BMW 730I SE	43735.00	-34653.79	9081.21	14695.00	5613.79	61.8%
3	05-Jul-94	26	CARINA E 1.6 GLI AUTO	24235.34	-19203.08	5032.26	4995.00	-37.27	-0.7%
4	11-Feb-95	33	AUDI 80 TDI	34682.77	-26223.76	8459.01	8495.00	35.99	0.4%
5	01-Aug-96	115	JAGUAR XJ12	53450.00	-33249.66	20200.34	7761.23	-12439.11	-61.6%
6	29-Nov-96	119	PASSAT 2.0 GL ESTATE	24313.28	-14483.50	9829.78	9995.00	165.22	1.7%
7	02-Jan-97	120	CAVALIER 1.8 CLASSIC	11840.00	-6845.00	4995.00	4995.00	0.00	0.0%
8	08-Jan-97	121	SAAB 9000I CSE EICOE 2.0 TURBO AUTO	27079.30	-15655.22	11424.08	11490.00	65.92	0.6%
9	24-Jan-97	122	AUDI A8 2.8 AUTO SALOON	36595.00	-21156.48	15438.52	25995.00	10556.48	68.4%
10	21-Feb-97	123	ROVER 111S	11372.61	-6441.52	4931.09	4995.00	63.90	1.3%
11	23-Feb-97	124	ROVER 218 STDI TURBO DIESEL	17015.59	-9637.74	7377.85	7495.00	117.15	1.6%
12	28-Feb-97	125	SAAB 900S COUPE	21720.56	-12302.66	9417.90	9595.00	177.10	1.9%
13	03-Mar-97	126	DISCOVERY TDI	30472.66	-16902.80	13569.86	13500.00	-69.86	-0.5%
14	03-Apr-97	127	GOLF CL 1.6	21606.58	-11731.70	9874.88	9795.00	-79.88	-0.8%
15	15-Apr-97	128	GOLF L	16390.98	-8899.79	7491.19	7495.00	3.81	0.1%
16	21-Apr-97	129	PEUGEOT 306 XRD 1.9	13035.38	-7077.80	5957.58	5995.00	37.42	0.6%
17	22-May-97	244	ALFA ROMEO CLOVER LEAF 24V	29557.27	-15702.30	13854.97	13950.00	95.03	0.7%
18	10-Jul-97	287	GOLF 1.4 CL	18359.01	-9322.93	9036.08	8995.00	-41.07	-0.5%
19	19-Jul-97	290	PROTON 1.6 SEI PERSONA	12039.73	-6113.93	5925.80	5950.00	24.19	0.4%
20	03-Aug-97	292	GOLF GTI 16V	26994.50	-13391.80	13602.70	13495.00	-107.69	-0.8%
21	18-Jan-98	311	TOYOTA COLORADO 1996 P REG	24999.00	-10937.06	14061.94	19995.00	5933.06	42.2%
22	25-Jan-98	312	ROVER 111 GSI	9922.60	-4341.14	5581.46	5695.00	113.54	2.0%
23	25-Jan-98	313	VAUXHALL TIGRA 1.4I	17946.05	-7851.40	10094.65	10300.00	205.34	2.0%
24	25-Mar-98	315	VAUXHALL ASTRA 1.6 PREMIER	11231.70	-4562.88	6668.82	6750.00	81.18	1.2%
25	07-Apr-98	316	RENAULT LAGUNA 3.0 V6	14804.25	-5782.91	9021.34	14661.80	5640.46	62.5%
26	18-May-98	324	ROVER 416I	11944.62	-4479.23	7465.39	7495.00	29.61	0.4%
27	26-May-98	325	VAUXHALL VECTRA 1.8 GLS SALOON	11083.83	-4156.44	6927.39	6995.00	67.61	1.0%
28	28-May-98	326	NISSAN PRIMERA 1.6 LX	9472.00	-3552.00	5920.00	5995.00	75.00	1.3%
29	12-Jun-98	332	GOLF GTI 16V	26994.50	-9701.15	17293.35	11995.00	-5298.35	-30.6%
30	14-Jun-98	334	MERCEDES BENZ C180 ELEGANCE	29307.62	-10532.43	18775.19	18950.00	174.80	0.9%
31	28-Jun-98	336	GOLF 1.4 SE	15123.84	-5435.13	9688.71	9795.00	106.29	1.1%
32	19-Jul-98	338	ROVER 214 SI	13650.93	-4692.51	8958.42	8995.00	36.57	0.4%
33	20-Jan-99	349	ROVER 420 SI SPORT	14450.64	-3612.66	10837.98	11199.25	361.27	3.3%
34	25-Feb-99	388	MERCEDES BENZ C180 ELEGANCE	29307.62	-6716.33	22591.29	23446.10	854.81	3.8%
35	28-Feb-99	390	SAAB 900S CONVERTIBLE	24569.33	-5630.47	18938.86	19655.46	716.60	3.8%
36	04-May-99	391	PEUGEOT 306 GTI 2.0	18130.34	-3021.72	15108.62	14957.53	-151.09	-1.0%
37	03-Oct-99	397	RENAULT LAGUNA 2.0 RT	11245.21	-702.83	10542.38	10682.95	140.57	1.3%
38									
39				768679.64	-384703.74	383975.90	397244.31	13268.42	
40									3.5%

Task 5

For the sake of clarity in presentation, some of the columns are not shown in the BPP solution.

Your check should reveal that the following assets have depreciation wrongly calculated by more than 10% of the amount currently provided. The formula used to do the recalculation is given in the question.

Code	Correct amount	Amount originally provided
32	105.47	140.50
43	501.16	804.16
254	96.30	69.20
291	73.07	7.17
323	234.69	323.00

Providing the depreciation for 2000 is straightforward. If you refer to the *Task 5* sheet in the DA7_S.xls file you will see the formulae we used. The first few rows are shown below.

	J	K	L
1	**Depn 2000**	**Cum Depn**	**NBV**
2	=G2*F2	=J2+H2	=G2-K2
3	=G3*F3	=J3+H3	=G3-K3
4	=G4*F4	=J4+H4	=G4-K4
5	=G5*F5	=J5+H5	=G5-K5
6	=G6*F6	=J6+H6	=G6-K6
7	=G7*F7	=J7+H7	=G7-K7
8	=G8*F8	=J8+H8	=G8-K8
9	=G9*F9	=J9+H9	=G9-K9
10	=G10*F10	=J10+H10	=G10-K10

The data for cars can be derived copied and pasted from your work for Task 4.

You should also have spotted the following points.

(a)   The following assets were already fully written down, and no depreciation should be provided in 2000.

    22   PC-386-25MHZ
    27   PRINTER
    105   PC-486-66MHZ
    106   PC-486-66MHZ
    107   PC-486-66MHZ
    108   PC-486-66MHZ
    109   PC-486-66MHZ
    110   PRINTER
    111   PRINTER
    112   PRINTER

(b)   The following assets should only be written down to nil in 2000. (In other words do not provide full depreciation or you will get negative balances.)

    113   TELEVISION
    288   PC-486-66MHZ
    289   PC-486-66MHZ

Here are the totals that we arrive at.

Cost price Dec 31 1999 £	Acc Depn to Dec 31 1999 £	NBV Dec 31 1999 £	Cost price Dec 31 2000 £	Depn charge Year 2000 £	Acc Depn to Dec 31 2000 £	NBV Dec 31 2000 £
1,317,127	462,790	854,337	1,350,155	140,258	603,048	747,107

Task 6

Your fixed assets note should look like this when you have extracted all the data.

	A	B Total £	C Land and buildings £	D Motor vehicles £	E Furniture and fittings £	F Office machinery £
1		Total	Land and buildings	Motor vehicles	Furniture and fittings	Office machinery
2		£	£	£	£	£
3	**Cost or valuation**					
4	At 1 January 2000	1,317,127	419,000	768,680	49,436	80,011
5	Additions in year	33,028		8,995	329	23,704
6	At 31 December 2000	1,350,155	419,000	777,675	49,765	103,715
7						
8	**Depreciation**					
9	At 1 January 2000	462,790	22,225	384,704	15,840	40,021
10	Charge for year	140,258	8,380	96,370	4,977	30,531
11	At 31 December 2000	603,048	30,605	481,074	20,817	70,552
12						
13	**Net book value**					
14	At 31 December 2000	747,107	388,395	296,601	28,948	33,163
15						
16	At 1 January 2000	854,337	396,775	383,976	33,596	39,990

You can extract the data very quickly using a Pivot Table and then transfer it into a sheet like this, or you can sort or filter the data by Asset category and collect separate sub-totals to paste into your final sheet.

Do not be surprised if your final figures are not exactly the same as the ones shown above. There are numerous opportunities for minor errors, rounding discrepancies, matters that can be treated in variety of ways, and so on. Congratulate yourself most of your answers have resembled ours.

Task 7

REPORT

To: Sarah Handley
From: Accounting Technician
Date: 4 January 2001

Subject: Executive Information Systems (EISs)

Introduction

As discussed, this report sets out some general information on types of information system and looks particularly at the possibility of setting up a Fixed Assets EIS to help with the management of fixed assets.

Types of information system

Transaction processing systems represent the lowest level in an organisation's use of information systems. They are used for routine tasks in which data items or transactions must be processed so that operations can continue. Processing sales orders, purchase orders, payroll items and stock records are typical examples.

Transaction processing systems provide the raw material which is often used more extensively to produce management information, such as reports on cumulative sales figures to date, value of current stock-in-hand, and so on.

Decision support system are computer systems designed to produce information that may help managers to make better decisions. DSS can describe a range of systems, from fairly simple information models based on spreadsheets to expert systems (described later).

Decision support systems do not make decisions. The objective is to allow the manager to consider a number of alternatives and evaluate them under a variety of potential conditions.

An Executive Information System (EIS) is a type of DSS that gives the 'executive' (ie a senior manager) easy access to key internal and external data in a user-friendly manner. An EIS is likely to have the following features.

(a) Provision of summary-level data, captured from the organisation's main systems.

(b) A facility which allows the executive to 'drill-down' from higher levels of information to lower.

(c) Data manipulation facilities (for example trend analysis).

(d) Graphics, for user-friendly presentation of data.

(e) A template system. This will mean that the same type of data is presented in the same format, irrespective of changes in the volume of information required.

Fixed Assets EIS

An EIS for asset management seems a desirable option, especially as we are in the business of insurance and would expect our own customers to keep reasonably well maintained records of the items they wish us to insure!

The EIS might offer features such as the following.

(a) A facility whereby each category of asset will *automatically* be depreciated in the accounts in a certain way. For example all assets recorded as computer equipment would be depreciated at 33.33% per annum on the straight line method.

(b) A separate record would be maintained for each asset. The record be an enhanced version of the records we keep at present and would contain information such as the following.

    (i) Asset number or code

    (ii) Company code, where a single register is maintained for a number of group companies

    (iii) Asset type, for example Motor Vehicles

    (iv) Department or cost centre using the asset, for example 'Product X Department - grinding'

    (v) A basic description of the asset, eg Toyota Corolla 2.0 GL

    (vi) Further identifying details, including any or all of the following.

        (1) Serial number

        (2) Engine number

        (3) Registration number

        (4) Colour

        (5) Details of extras or enhancements (a leather top on a desk, a car alarm etc)

        (6) Key/lock numbers, especially for cars, desk drawers and filing cabinets.

    (vii) Date of purchase

    (viii) Purchase price

(ix) Name of supplier

(x) The location of the asset

(xi) The name of the person responsible for it (especially in the case of a car)

(xii) The insured value

(xiii) Estimated asset life and residual value

(xiv) Details of maintenance contracts, user support telephone numbers and the like

(c) The system might allow for assets to be *transferred* in various ways. A company car may be passed from one salesperson to another, for instance, but we have no records of this at present. Increasingly companies are using *bar codes* on smaller assets so that when an asset audit is being carried out the auditor simply needs to scan the bar code on each asset as it is encountered and key codes for current location and so on into a hand-held device.

(d) The system should also be capable of recording *disposal* details, such as the name of the buyer of the asset and the disposal proceeds received or part exchange value agreed. In the case of part exchanges it is useful to have a record of which new asset the old one was exchanged for. Our records do not contain any details of disposals at all.

(e) The system should be able to produce a wide variety of reports on any aspect of the information it contains.

(f) Asset maintenance records might record diary details of work done (or mileage clocked up or whatever) to date and details of maintenance to be carried out once a certain period has elapsed (for example, an annual check of electrical safety) or after so many thousands of miles or hours of use. This can be used to plan out maintenance programmes in advance.

(g) Vehicle fleet management records would include all of the above facilities and should also have records of *drivers* - ages, mileage, accident records, type of licence held (eg HGV, motorbike) - and fuel usage, both by car and by driver. Fuel is a significant expense for many companies and consumption should be carefully monitored. Some systems even have journey planners that can provide a print-out showing and describing the quickest route from A to B, and so helping to cut fuel costs and journey time.

(h) The systems might also offer some sort of capital budgeting facility which records and controls expenditure on assets.

A full scale system such as described above may be beyond the current needs of the business, but I hope that it has given you food for thought on how the present system could be improved.

Password

The password to open the BPP solution is **PRU**

AAT Sample Simulation

AAT sample simulation
8 Koolfoot

Performance criteria

The following performance criteria are covered in this simulation.

Element 21.1

Obtain information from a computerised Management Information System

1   The required information is correctly located within the MIS structure

4   Information is checked for its accuracy and completeness

5   Information is stored in a format which helps others to access it and use it

Element 21.2

Produce spreadsheets for the analysis of numerical information

1   The spreadsheet is titled in a way which clearly defines its use and purpose

2   The arrangement of the spreadsheet is consistent with organisational conventions

3   All rates and other numeric inputs and assumptions are stated to the correct number of decimal places

4   Calculated values are checked for correctness when changes are made to the inputs

5   The spreadsheet is used to carry out data modifications and for entry of related formulas

6   Each cell is formatted clearly and accurately

Element 21.3

Contribute to the quality of the Management Information System

1   Potential improvements to the MIS are identified and considered for their impact on the quality of the system and any interrelated systems

2   Suggestions for changes are supported by a clear rationale as to how they could improve the quality of the system

3   The reliability of assumptions and judgements made is assessed and clearly stated

4   The benefits and costs of all changes are described accurately

5   Suggestions are presented clearly and in a way which helps people to understand and act on them

Notes on completing the Simulation

This simulation is designed to test your ability to use a management information system.

The situation and tasks are set out for you on pages **155** to **157**.

You are allowed **4 hours** to complete your work.

A high level of accuracy is required. Check your work carefully.

Any spreadsheet that you create should be in good form with proper formatting and making use of a full range of facilities offered. You will not be penalised if the hardware and software tht you use are not the very latest versions. It will not count against you if, for example, you do not have a colour printer or your package does not contain multiple pages.

Attention should be paid to the presentation of your output and reports. You should make full use of the printing facilties, for exmple to make sure that you include proper titles and include headers and footers where appropriate.

Any computer files that are presented for assessment should be on a floppy disk that is clearly marked with your name, the fact that the disk is part of an AAT simulation and the name of the responsible tutor. You should also list the names of the the files on the disk. Filenames should give some indication of their content.

You may either present your answers to the written tasks in handwritten form or as a word processed document if you wish. If you hand write, correcting fluid may be used but it should be used in moderation. Errors should be crossed out neatly and clearly. You should write in black ink, not pencil.

You are advised to read the whole simulation before commencing as all information may be of value and is not necessarly supplied in the sequence in which you would wish to deal with it.

A full solution to this Assessment is provided on page 161. Do not turn to the suggested solution until you have completed all parts of the Assessment.

AAT SAMPLE SIMULATION: KOOLFOOT

The situation

Introduction

When Jane Jones inherited the family shoe shop in November 1998, she made some dramatic changes. She could see that the business was no longer able to compete with the national chains and so reorganised the business completely. She got rid of the traditional wide range of shoes of all styles and, for all age groups, replaced them with a range of training shoes. She redesigned the shop and changed the name to KoolFoot. She decided to specialise in a limited range of high-quality trainers from four of the major manufacturers with a strategy of buying in bulk to keep down the costs of purchases and passing on the savings to her customers. The objective is to achieve a high volume of sales to strengthen her negotiating position with her suppliers.

The business is currently a small one, operating from a shop of 150 square metres in a small market town. Jane hopes to prove that her business ideas are sound and then to expand into neighbouring towns as soon as possible. She employs two full time assistants and manages the shop herself. From her observations and from the cash-flow generated in the first full year of trading in the new manner, she is convinced that she will succeed.

It is now the end of March 2000 and KoolFoot is at the end of the first full year's trading. Jane is getting ready to send her financial records to her accountant for accounts to be prepared. She knows that you are training to be an accounting technician and have some knowledge about how to use information technology and has asked you to help with getting some of the information together with regard to sales and stock levels.

The stock and stock records

The shop specialises in the following brands of trainers.

> Hike
>
> Oddidos
>
> Panther
>
> NY Gear

and offers nine styles from each manufacturer. It uses the European shoe sizes, and each size is stocked for boys and girls and alternate sizes for men and women.

The sizes stocked are shown in the table below.

Boys-size	26	Girls-size	26
	27		27
	28		28
	29		29
	30		30
	31		31
	32		32
	33	Womens-size	34
	34		36
	35		38
	36		40
	37		42
Mens-size	38		44
	40		
	42		
	44		
	46		
	48		

BPP PUBLISHING

Jane has kept stock records on a spreadsheet and these are available with the BPP data under the file name

DA8_Q

The spreadsheet is based on a simple coding system that indicates the important details of the stock and shows the position at 28 March 2000.

The first character is

H	for	Hike
O	for	Oddidos
P	for	Panther
N	for	NY Gear.

The next character (1 to 9) indicates the style, the next character is a B, M, G or W for boy, man, girl or woman and the code terminates with the shoe size. Thus H2W34 indicates a Hike shoe, in style 2 and is a woman's shoe, size 34. N8B36 is a NY Gear shoe, in style 8, for a boy and size 36.

Jane has updated her stock every week and has consolidated the data on to the **DA8_Q** spreadsheet. An extract is printed below.

Count	Product Code	Opening stock	Sales	Deliveries
1	H1B26	1	0	1
2	H1B27	1	1	1
3	H1B28	1	1	1
4	H1B29	2	2	2
5	H1B30	0	2	2
6	H1B31	2	1	1
7	H1B32	0	1	1
8	H1B33	1	2	2
9	H1B34	0	1	1
10	H1B35	2	3	3
11	H1B36	0	2	2
12	H1B37	1	2	3
13	H1M38	0	5	5

Your Role

Jane is very busy with the day to day management of the shop and has asked you to carry out some analysis of her figures to assist her in providing year end information for her accountant and to give her a better insight into the way the business is working. The tasks are set out in the next section and you should carry these out in such a way that you can hand over to her a package of material (modified spreadsheets, notes, reports etc.) that she can take home and work on in the evening.

TASKS TO BE COMPLETED

1. Load Jane's spreadsheet filename **DA8_Q** and improve its general appearance and readability by adding titles and formats as you see fit.

2. Add a column to show the expected closing stock.

3. Your list of closing balances should show up some negative balances.

   Write a brief informal report for Jane that:

   • Identifies the negative balances

- Suggests how they might have arisen
- Discusses their implications

4. Use your closing stock figures to create a column which shows stock turnover figures for each product.

   (*Note.* You have discussed how to calculate stock turnover with Jane and have agreed that the most appropriate method is to divide the total sales figure for the year by the average of stock held at the beginning and the end of the year.)

5. Jane would like to use the spreadsheet as a basis for quarterly stocktaking. In order to see how viable this is she would like you to create a new version of **DA8_Q** which provides a list of stock items that the staff can use to enter actual stock levels. Save this new file to floppy disk and print two pages of this spreadsheet as a sample of your proposed stocktaking record.

6. Jane feels that she ought to be able to use the spreadsheet to help her understand the sales pattern in the business. She believes that she has only a limited understanding of the importance of the various lines and would like to get a better feel for what is happening. She is even aware that she does not know which are the right questions to ask.

   In your discussions with Jane you have explained that a spreadsheet is not the best tool for this analysis but you have agreed to try to help.

   It has been decided that your task is to investigate the sales patterns by looking just at the styles from one manufacturer (Hike) and to write a note for Jane that:

   - Provides her with some insight into the sales pattern (for example the relative importance of the childrens' and adults' ranges, the relative importance of mens' and womens' styles and the distribution of sizes)

   - Provides her with some information about which lines she should concentrate on in the future and which she should consider dropping

   - Identifies the problems involved in making a decision to delete a product line on the basis of information presented in the spreadsheet

7. Jane feels that although she has a flair for retailing, she lacks any formal understanding of management information systems.

   She would like you to write a brief formal report about the nature of management information relating to stock (inventory) management in her business. The purpose of this report is firstly to raise issues for her to think about and eventually to form the basis of her discussions with a firm of management consultants who will be asked to install a full electronic point of sales system when the business expands.

   The areas that she would like you to cover are:

   - The various aspects of the management task (operational, tactical and strategic) as they relate to her as owner/manager

   - The type of information that would help her to perform these tasks well

   - Practical ways in which she could provide the information that you have identified in the context of this business

Solution to AAT Sample Simulation

SOLUTION TO AAT SAMPLE DEVOLVED ASSESSMENT: KOOLFOOT

Solution

For a full suggested answer look at the BPP file **DA8_S**. The password to open this spreadsheet is given later in this solution.

Task 1

You should have provided some form of heading for the spreadsheet to explain its purpose.

You should have tidied up the column headings and aligned them with the data.

Your spreadsheet should look something like this.

	A	B	C	D	E	F	G	H	I
1					Stocklist as at 28th March				
2									
3	Count	Maker	Style	B/M/G/W	Size	Product	Opening	Sales	Deliveries
4						Code	Stock		
5	1	H	1	B	26	H1B26	1	0	1
6	2	H	1	B	27	H1B27	1	1	1
7	3	H	1	B	28	H1B28	1	1	1
8	4	H	1	B	29	H1B29	2	2	2
9	5	H	1	B	30	H1B30	0	2	2
10	6	H	1	B	31	H1B31	2	1	1
11	7	H	1	B	32	H1B32	0	1	1
12	8	H	1	B	33	H1B33	1	2	2
13	9	H	1	B	34	H1B34	0	1	1
14	10	H	1	B	35	H1B35	2	3	3
15	11	H	1	B	36	H1B36	0	2	2

The extra column showing each **Product Code** in a single cell (which is potentially useful for any further analysis of the data) can be generated in a number of ways.

(a) In recent versions of Excel by using the formula =B3&C3&D3&E3.

(b) By selecting columns B to E, copying them, pasting them into a text editor such as Microsoft Word, converting the resulting table to text, removing extra characters (probably tabs) by means of a search and replace, and then copying and pasting the data back into a single column (column E above). (This is less laborious than it sounds. To find and replace a tab character in Microsoft Word use ^t.)

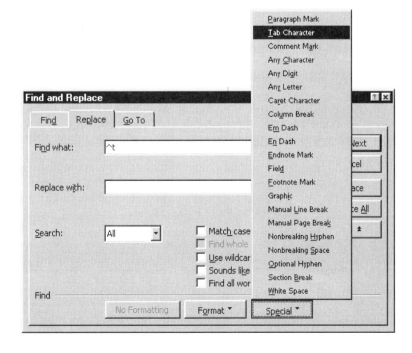

BPP
PUBLISHING

(c)   By typing H1B26 in cell F5 and filling down with the mouse to enter the other H1B.. codes, then typing H1M and filling down, and so on. This is a fairly laborious method and would need to be checked carefully for input errors.

Task 2

The formula to use in cell J5 (if your spreadsheet is laid out like ours) is =G5-H5+I5. You can then fill down with the mouse to complete the other rows.

	A	B	C	D	E	F	G	H	I	J
1				Stocklist as at 28th March						
2										
3	Count	Maker	Style	B/M/G/W	Size	Product	Opening	Sales	Deliveries	Closing
4						Code	Stock			Stock
5	1	H	1	B	26	H1B26	1	0	1	=G5-H5+I5
6	2	H	1	B	27	H1B27	1	1	1	1
7	3	H	1	B	28	H1B28	1	1	1	1
8	4	H	1	B	29	H1B29	2	2	2	2

If your first row is correct, all the others should be too. However, if you wish to check every row of your own answer you can copy the closing stock column from our answer, paste it in into your spreadsheet (*using the* **Paste Special ... Values** *option*) and then subtract your column from ours in the next column. The answer should be zero for each line unless you have made an error, so the column as a whole should sum to zero.

Task 3

Tutorial note. In Excel you can use the **Data ... Filter ... Auto Filter** to identify negative balances, and copy and paste them into a new spreadsheet once you have found them. There are only three, as shown in our answer below.

Alternatively, but just as effectively, you could **Sort** the data in ascending numerical order, on the **Closing Stock** column.

Alternatively you could use a formula in another column such as =IF(J5<0,"Error","OK") and then fill down the other rows. This makes the negative balances stand out more as you scroll through the list. To be sure you had found them all you could do a **Find** for "Error".

REPORT

To: Jane Jones
From: Accounting Technician
Date: 31 March 2000

Negative Stock Balances

An analysis of your stock records spreadsheet reveals that the following products have negative values for stock as at 28 March 2000. A negative balance is, of course, impossible because we are dealing with physical items.

Negative Stock balances									
Count	Maker	Style	B/M/G/W	Size	Product	Opening	Sales	Deliveries	Closing
					Code	Stock			Stock
25	H	1	G	32	H1G32	0	2	1	-1
88	H	7	G	26	H7G26	0	11	10	-1
161	O	5	G	29	O5G29	0	11	10	-1

These errors may have arisen for a number of reasons.

(a)   Because of an error in recording the opening stock figure.

(b)   Because of an error in recording sales of these items.

(c)   Because of an error in recording delivery quantities.

(d)   Because sales of other products have been incorrectly allocated to these products.

(e)   Because the records have been deliberately manipulated in some way, for instance in an attempt to cover up theft of stock.

The only obvious pattern to the errors discovered so far is that each item with a negative balance is a girl's shoe. It may be worth considering whether records for these have been dealt with differently (for instance entered by a different person) from other shoes.

Although errors have only been definitely identified in three product records (less than 1% of the total) the existence of three clear errors implies that there may be **many further errors** which have not yet been detected. For instance the spreadsheet may show closing stock for an item as 4, whereas in reality there are 3 or 5 items in stock. Such a discrepancy could arise for any of the reasons stated above.

Only a full and careful **count of physical stock** will reveal the extent of such errors. I strongly recommend that such a count is made as soon as possible. Meanwhile records of sales and deliveries for the three items identified above should be investigated to see if the errors can be traced.

Task 4

You are instructed to calculate stock turnover as Sales/(Opening Stock + Closing Stock/2). This is therefore exactly what you should do, even though you may feel that it is not completely appropriate.

To avoid a "Divide by 0" error, we have included an **if** statement in our answer, as follows.

=IF((J5+G5)/2=0,"",(H5/((J5+G5)/2)))

This gives blank cells where opening and closing stock is zero. In such cases stock turnover is **really** either 1.00 (if there was no opening or closing stock and all deliveries have been sold: eg item H1B30) or 0.00 (if the item has not been in stock, sold or delivered all year eg item H5W44). It is merely coincidence that stocks were nil on the opening and closing days. A better formula might be =IF((J5+G5)/2=0,(H5/I5),(H5/((J5+G5)/2))).

Score bonus marks if you pointed this out in your answer. However, you **must** use the calculation method prescribed in the instructions. If you simply used a formula like =H5/((J5+G5)/2) you should get full marks.

Here are the first few lines of our answer, with the formula shown in cell K5. We have formatted column K to show the figures to 2 decimal places.

163

	A	B	C	D	E	F	G	H	I	J	K
1						Stocklist as at 28th March					
2											
3	Count	Maker	Style	B/M/G/W	Size	Product	Opening	Sales	Deliveries	Closing	Stock
4						Code	Stock			Stock	Turnover
5	1	H	1	B	26	H1B26	1	0	1	2	=IF((J5+G5)/2=0,"",(H5/((J5+G5)/2)))
6	2	H	1	B	27	H1B27	1	1	1	1	1.00
7	3	H	1	B	28	H1B28	1	1	1	1	1.00
8	4	H	1	B	29	H1B29	2	2	2	2	1.00
9	5	H	1	B	30	H1B30	0	2	2	0	
10	6	H	1	B	31	H1B31	2	1	1	2	0.50
11	7	H	1	B	32	H1B32	0	1	1	0	
12	8	H	1	B	33	H1B33	1	2	2	1	2.00
13	9	H	1	B	34	H1B34	0	1	1	0	
14	10	H	1	B	35	H1B35	2	3	3	2	1.50
15	11	H	1	B	36	H1B36	0	2	2	0	
16	12	H	1	B	37	H1B37	1	2	3	2	1.33
17	13	H	1	M	38	H1M38	0	5	5	0	
18	14	H	1	M	40	H1M40	0	6	10	4	3.00
19	15	H	1	M	42	H1M42	1	19	20	2	12.67
20	16	H	1	M	44	H1M44	1	15	20	6	4.29
21	17	H	1	M	46	H1M46	0	5	5	0	
22	18	H	1	M	48	H1M48	1	11	10	0	22.00
23	19	H	1	G	26	H1G26	0	2	2	0	
24	20	H	1	G	27	H1G27	1	2	3	2	1.33
25	21	H	1	G	28	H1G28	1	2	2	1	2.00
26	22	H	1	G	29	H1G29	1	2	3	2	1.33
27	23	H	1	G	30	H1G30	1	1	1	1	1.00
28	24	H	1	G	31	H1G31	1	1	2	2	0.67
29	25	H	1	G	32	H1G32	0	2	1	-1	-4.00
30	26	H	1	W	34	H1W34	1	4	5	2	2.67

Task 5

Below are shown the first two pages of our solution as they would appear when printed out. Note the following points.

(a)   The only information needed to allow the stock take to be completed is the product code. Balances **should not** be included because counters might then be tempted to enter the same figure as shown in the records rather than doing a proper count.

(b)   A space should be provided for the person who completed each sheet to enter their name and the date.

(c)   Space for entry of numbers and comments should be more than adequate to encourage clear handwriting. (We use a row height of 36.)

(d)   Headings should be repeated at the top of each page (for instance in Excel use **Page Setup ... Sheet ... Rows to repeat at top**).

(e)   Each page should have an indication of its page number and the total number of pages ("Page 1 of 27" in our example). You can set up the spreadsheet to include this information automatically when printed out, for instance using the **Page Setup ... Header Footer** options.

	Stocktake List	

Date _____

Completed by _____

Product Code	Count	Comments
H1B26		
H1B27		
H1B28		
H1B29		
H1B30		
H1B31		
H1B32		
H1B33		
H1B34		
H1B35		
H1B36		
H1B37		

Page 1 of 27

BPP
PUBLISHING

Stocktake List		

Date _____

Completed by _____

Product Code	Count	Comments
H1M38		
H1M40		
H1M42		
H1M44		
H1M46		
H1M48		
H1G26		
H1G27		
H1G28		
H1G29		
H1G30		
H1G31		
Page 2 of 27		

Task 6

The following patterns emerge from an analysis of the sales data for Hike shoes.

Sales by sex and age

Boys shoes	83
Girls shoes	140
Men's shoes	597
Women's shoes	<u>279</u>
Total sales of Hike shoes	1,099

Comment: Adult shoe sales make up more than three quarters of the total. More than twice as many men's shoes are sold as women's shoes. However, more girl's shoes are sold than boy's shoes.

It may be worth considering ceasing to sell children's shoes, assuming that sales could be made up by selling more adult shoes, or that the cost of maintaining stocks and a service for children outweighs the sales income derived from children's shoes. However, an alternative may be to lower the price of children's shoes, or stock a lower quality brand, since parents will typically be reluctant to pay premium prices for high quality shoes when they know that their children are going to outgrow them in a few months.

It is also necessary to consider whether dropping children's shoes may have a knock-on effect on sales of adult shoes. Young customers will of course get older, and it may be worth starting to build up customer loyalty at an early age. Some adult customers may wish to take advantage of the fact that they can currently buy shoes for all the family in one shop.

Sales by size, and by sex and age

Size	Sales	Sex/Age	Sales
26	23	B	3
		G	20
27	25	B	5
		G	20
28	20	B	3
		G	17
29	28	B	6
		G	22
30	27	B	7
		G	20
31	26	B	7
		G	19
32	27	B	5
		G	22
33	8	B	8
34	35	B	7
		W	28
35	12	B	12
36	60	B	11
		W	49
37	9	B	9
38	152	M	54
		W	98
40	138	M	72
		W	66
42	209	M	183
		W	26
44	143	M	131
		W	12
46	54	M	54
48	103	M	103

Sales in order of size		
M	42	183
M	44	131
M	48	103
W	38	98
M	40	72
W	40	66
M	38	54
M	46	54
W	36	49
W	34	28
W	42	26
G	29	22
G	32	22
G	26	20
G	27	20
G	30	20
G	31	19
G	28	17
B	35	12
W	44	12
B	36	11
B	37	9
B	33	8
B	30	7
B	31	7
B	34	7
B	29	6
B	27	5
B	32	5
B	26	3
B	28	3

Comment: Most men take a shoe size of 42 or slightly smaller or slightly larger. Most women take a shoe size of 38 or slightly smaller or slightly larger.

Children's shoes sell in about the same numbers for each size. This is to be expected as children's feet are still growing.

Stocks of the most common sizes should be maintained at a higher level than for other sizes. There is possibly a case for ceasing to stock the smallest boy's sizes and the largest women's sizes. Alternatively the business may wish to continue to provide a full range of products in all sizes (even if limited stocks are available) as a service that will be valued by customers and possibly earn customer loyalty and repeat business.

Sales by style

Style 8 (M)	324
Style 6 (M)	212
Style 7 (G/W)	177
Style 1 (B/G/M/W)	133
Style 9 (G/W)	84
Style 2 (G/W)	75
Style 3 (B)	37
Style 5 (G/W)	29
Style 4 (B)	28
Total	1,099

Comment: Styles 8 and 6 are the most popular men's style. Style 7 is the most popular girl's/women's style. Style 1's apparent popularity is accounted for by the fact that it is available across all ages and sexes, whereas style 3, for instance is only available for boys.

It may be worth considering dropping styles 3, 4 and 5. On the other hand, styles 3 and 4 together make up the majority of sales of boy's shoes.

Nil sales

Products H1B26 (a very small boy's shoe) and H5W44 (a very large women's shoe) have nil sales.

If you are using Microsoft Excel, much of the above data can be extracted in one go by creating a pivot table as follows.

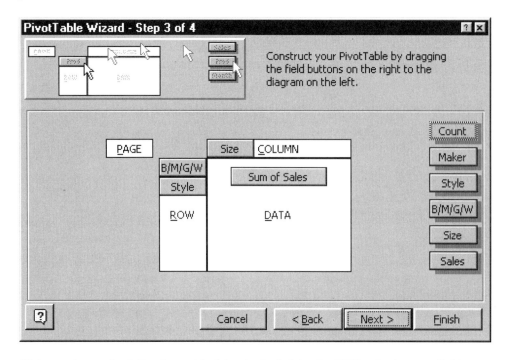

This produces the following table (also included in the BPP solution on disk).

Sum of Sales		Size																		
B/M/G/W	Style	26	27	28	29	30	31	32	33	34	35	36	37	38	40	42	44	46	48	Grand Total
B	1	0	1	1	2	2	1	1	2	1	3	2	2							18
	3	2	2	1	3	3	3	2	3	4	5	5	4							37
	4	1	2	1	1	2	3	2	3	2	4	4	3							28
B Total		3	5	3	6	7	7	5	8	7	12	11	9							83
G	1	2	2	2	2	1	1	2												12
	2	3	4	3	4	4	4	3												25
	5	1	1	1	2	1	1	2												9
	7	11	10	8	10	10	9	11												69
	9	3	3	3	4	4	4	4												25
G Total		20	20	17	22	20	19	22												140
M	1													5	6	19	15	5	11	61
	6													20	29	52	51	18	42	212
	8													29	37	112	65	31	50	324
M Total														54	72	183	131	54	103	597
W	1									4		8		13	12	3	2			42
	2									5		9		18	12	4	2			50
	5									1		4		8	5	2	0			20
	7									12		20		35	25	10	6			108
	9									6		8		24	12	7	2			59
W Total										28		49		98	66	26	12			279
Grand Total		23	25	20	28	27	26	27	8	35	12	60	9	152	138	209	143	54	103	1099

If you do not have this feature the best approach is to extract the following data onto a separate sheet and sort it in a variety of ways.

	A	B	C	D	E	F
1	Count	Maker	Style	B/M/G/W	Size	Sales
2	1	H	1	B	26	0
3	2	H	1	B	27	1
4	3	H	1	B	28	1
5	4	H	1	B	29	2
6	5	H	1	B	30	2
7	6	H	1	B	31	1
8	7	H	1	B	32	1
9	8	H	1	B	33	2

Task 7

REPORT

To: Jane Jones
From: Accounting Technician
Date: 31 March 2000

Subject: Management information

This report examines the nature of management information, especially as it relates to stock management in your business.

The management task and information needs

Information necessary to help people make decisions within a business can be analysed into three levels: *strategic, tactical, and operational.*

Strategic information is used to plan the long-term objectives of the organisation, and to assess whether the objectives are being met in practice. This information includes overall profitability, the profitability of different 'segments' of the business (for instance different branches of a shop), future market prospects, the availability and cost of raising new funds, total cash needs, total manning levels and capital equipment needs, if any.

Strategic information is derived from both internal and external sources. It is never absolutely certain, given that the future cannot be predicted. A good example would be an article in a retail trade magazine about trends within the shoe retailing business covering the popularity of different shoe manufacturers and the performance of competing retailers.

Strategic decisions would include decisions about whether to open more branches or whether to sell other outdoor wear besides shoes, for example.

Tactical information is used to decide how the resources of the business should be employed, and to monitor how they are being and have been employed. This information includes productivity measurements (sales per shoe shop assistant), budgetary control, cash flow forecasts, profit results within a particular part of the business (for instance profits on Hike as opposed to profits on Oddidos shoes).

Tactical information relates to the short to medium term (eg the next month or the next 'season'). Tactical decisions made on the basis of such information might include decisions about the pricing of products, decisions on what range of sizes and styles to stock, decisions about bonus schemes to motivate shop-floor staff.

Operational information is used for the day to day management of the business to ensure that specific tasks are planned and carried out properly.

Operational information relates to the immediate term. Decisions would include day to day tasks such as working out what items of stock are low and need re-ordering each day; or whether there is enough cash in the till; or whether a staff member could be allowed to take a long lunch hour on a particular day.

Ways of providing the information

At present the business consists of one shop, managed personally by the owner of the business, with two staff. It stocks nine lines of shoe from each of four manufacturers: 36 items in total.

In view of this an extremely complex system of information provision is quite unjustified. Information collection can be relatively informal: for instance stock levels can be determined more or less by means of a glance round the stock room, if the stock room itself is large enough to store things in a well-organised fashion.

Using a spreadsheet to keep account of stock movements is also a perfectly acceptable and sensible approach at this level of business.

However, if the intention is to expand the business there will come a point when it is not possible to supervise every aspect of the business personally and a more sophisticated system is needed both to maintain control ad to keep down the administrative workload.

You have mentioned the possibility of installing an electronic point of sale system (EPOS), and this would certainly be a good idea as the business grows. You have no doubt seen these in action, for instance in supermarkets. The customer buys bar coded items and takes them to the checkout to pay. The shop assistant uses a bar code reader which transmits the bar coded data to a central processor in the store. The computer then provides the price of the item being purchased (from a price list held on the stock file) and this is output to the cashier's check-out point.

At the same time, the data about the purchases that have been read into the computer from the bar codes can be used to update the stock file and record the sales data for management information purposes.

Electronic Point of Sale (EPOS) devices act both as cash registers and as terminals connected to a main computer. This enables the computer to produce useful management information such as sales details and analysis and stock control information very quickly. The provision of immediate sales information (for example, which products sell quickly), perhaps analysed on a branch basis, permits great speed and flexibility in decision-making (certainly of a short-term nature), as customers wishes can be responded to quickly.

Conclusion

Though desirable an EPOS may be a relatively expensive option at present. It may be worth discussing your needs with your bankers or with your suppliers. They may offer special deals on systems that incorporate EPOS technology and link in with their own systems.

Password

The password to open the BPP solution is **Adidas**

BPP PUBLISHING

ORDER FORM

Any books from our AAT range can be ordered by telephoning 020-8740-2211. Alternatively, send this page to our address below, fax it to us on 020-8740-1184, or email us at **publishing@bpp.com.** Or look us up on our website: www.bpp.com

We aim to deliver to all UK addresses inside 5 working days; a signature will be required. Order to all EU addresses should be delivered within 6 working days. All other orders to overseas addresses should be delivered within 8 working days.

To: BPP Publishing Ltd, Aldine House, Aldine Place, London W12 8AW

Tel: 020-8740 2211   **Fax: 020-8740 1184**   **Email: publishing@bpp.com**

Mr / Ms (full name): _____

Daytime delivery address: _____

_____

Postcode: _____   Daytime Tel: _____

Please send me the following quantities of books.

	5/00 Interactive Text	8/00 DA Kit	8/00 CA Kit
FOUNDATION			
Unit 1 Recording Income and Receipts (7/00 Text)	☐	☐	
Unit 2 Making and Recording Payments (7/00 Text)	☐	☐	
Unit 3 Ledger Balances and Initial Trial Balance (7/00 Text)	☐		☐
Unit 4 Supplying information for Management Control (6/00 Text)	☐	☐	
Unit 20 Working with Information Technology (8/00 Text)	☐		
Unit 22/23 Achieving Personal Effectiveness (7/00) Text	☐		
INTERMEDIATE			
Unit 5 Financial Records and Accounts	☐		☐
Unit 6 Cost Information	☐		
Unit 7 Reports and Returns	☐	☐	
Unit 21 Using Information Technology	☐		
Unit 22: see below			
TECHNICIAN			
Unit 8/9 Core Managing Costs and Allocating Resources	☐		
Unit 10 Core Managing Accounting Systems	☐	☐	
Unit 11 Option Financial Statements (Accounting Practice)	☐		☐
Unit 12 Option Financial Statements (Central Government)	☐		
Unit 15 Option Cash Management and Credit Control	☐	☐	
Unit 16 Option Evaluating Activities	☐		
Unit 17 Option Implementing Auditing Procedures	☐		
Unit 18 Option Business Tax FA00(8/00 Text)	☐	☐	
Unit 19 Option Personal Tax FA00(8/00 Text)	☐		
TECHNICIAN 1999			
Unit 17 Option Business Tax Computations FA99 (8/99 Text & Kit)	☐	☐	
Unit 18 Option Personal Tax Computations FA99 (8/99 Text & Kit)	☐	☐	
TOTAL BOOKS	☐ +	☐ +	☐ = ☐

@ £9.95 each = £ ☐

Postage and packaging:

UK: £2.00 for each book to maximum of £10

Europe (inc ROI and Channel Islands): £4.00 for first book, £2.00 for each extra   P & P   £ ☐

Rest of the World: £20.00 for first book, £10 for each extra

► Unit 22 Maintaining a Healthy Workplace Interactive Text (postage free)   ☐ @ £3.95   £ ☐

GRAND TOTAL £ ☐

I enclose a cheque for £ _____ (cheques to BPP Publishing Ltd) or charge to Mastercard/Visa/Switch

Card number ☐☐☐☐ ☐☐☐☐ ☐☐☐☐ ☐☐☐☐ ☐☐☐☐ ☐☐☐☐

Start date _____   **Expiry date** _____   **Issue no. (Switch only)**___

Signature _____

REVIEW FORM & FREE PRIZE DRAW

All original review forms from the entire BPP range, completed with genuine comments, will be entered into one of two draws on 31 January 2001 and 31 July 2001. The names on the first four forms picked out on each occasion will be sent a cheque for £50.

Name: _____   Address: _____

_____

_____

How have you used this Devolved Assessment Kit?
(Tick one box only)

☐ Home study (book only)

☐ On a course: college _____

☐ With 'correspondence' package

☐ Other _____

Why did you decide to purchase this Devolved Assessment Kit? *(Tick one box only)*

☐ Have used BPP Texts in the past

☐ Recommendation by friend/colleague

☐ Recommendation by a lecturer at college

☐ Saw advertising

☐ Other _____

During the past six months do you recall seeing/receiving any of the following?
(Tick as many boxes as are relevant)

☐ Our advertisement in *Accounting Technician* magazine

☐ Our advertisement in *Pass*

☐ Our brochure with a letter through the post

Which (if any) aspects of our advertising do you find useful?
(Tick as many boxes as are relevant)

☐ Prices and publication dates of new editions

☐ Information on Interactive Text content

☐ Facility to order books off-the-page

☐ None of the above

Have you used the companion Assessment Kits for this subject?   ☐ Yes   ☐ No

Your ratings, comments and suggestions would be appreciated on the following areas

	Very useful	Useful	Not useful
Introductory section (How to use this Devolved Assessment Kit etc)	☐	☐	☐
Practice Activities	☐	☐	☐
Practice Devolved Assessments	☐	☐	☐
Trial Run Devolved Assessments	☐	☐	☐
AAT Sample Simulation	☐	☐	☐
Content of Answers	☐	☐	☐
Layout of pages	☐	☐	☐
Structure of book and ease of use	☐	☐	☐

	Excellent	Good	Adequate	Poor
Overall opinion of this Kit	☐	☐	☐	☐

Do you intend to continue using BPP Assessment Kits/Interactive Texts/? ☐ Yes   ☐ No

Please note any further comments and suggestions/errors on the reverse of this page.

Please return to: Nick Weller, BPP Publishing Ltd, FREEPOST, London, W12 8BR

REVIEW FORM & FREE PRIZE DRAW (continued)

Please note any further comments and suggestions/errors below

FREE PRIZE DRAW RULES

1   Closing date for 31 January 2001 draw is 31 December 2000. Closing date for 31 July 2001 draw is 30 June 2001.

2   Restricted to entries with UK and Eire addresses only. BPP employees, their families and business associates are excluded.

3   No purchase necessary. Entry forms are available upon request from BPP Publishing. No more than one entry per title, per person. Draw restricted to persons aged 16 and over.

4   Winners will be notified by post and receive their cheques not later than 6 weeks after the relevant draw date.

5   The decision of the promoter in all matters is final and binding. No correspondence will be entered into.